The Dawning...

Facing God "Head On"

Linda Luz Benvenue

Note for Librarians: A cataloging record for this book is available from Library and Archives Canada at www.collectionscanada.ca/amicus/index-e.html

ISBN: 978-1-4251-2854-8

We at Trafford believe that it is the responsibility of us all, as both individuals and corporations, to make choices that are environmentally and socially sound. You, in turn, are supporting this responsible conduct each time you purchase a Trafford book, or make use of our publishing services. To find out how you are helping, please visit www.trafford.com/responsiblepublishing.html

Our mission is to efficiently provide the world's finest, most comprehensive book publishing service, enabling every author to experience success.

www.trafford.com

North America & international
toll-free: 1 888 232 4444 (USA & Canada)
phone: 250 383 6864 ♦ fax: 250 383 6804 ♦ email: info@trafford.com

The United Kingdom & Europe
phone: +44 (0)1865 722 113 ♦ local rate: 0845 230 9601
facsimile: +44 (0)1865 722 868 ♦ email: info.uk@trafford.com

10 9 8 7 6 5 4 3 2

Acknowledgements

To everyone who touched my life, thank you. This book is a retelling of events that happened to me that never would have been possible had you not made an appearance in my life, no matter how brief.

Reflecting back, your presence helped shape my days in ways you may not have been aware of. From you I learned how to appropriately accept and respond to love, to choose peace over pandemonium, graciousness over rudeness, stillness over movement, patience over impulsiveness, and most importantly, to listen over idle chatter.

When I was ready you guided me in the ways of religious faith and pointed the road to spiritual liberation. While the former fed my mind, the latter enlivened my spirit giving expression to the Divine within me. Because of your attentiveness, I've come to know the importance of giving proper thought to that part of me that is transient and that which is never ending. Because of the latter, I'm aware that I'm living a part of eternity right now.

Finally, to my husband, who gave me courage to define who I am without pretense and who lovingly supported me in this effort, and to my three wonderful children, who were placed in my life according to the Divine plan laid out for me. I want you to know that your place in my life was not coincidental; it was Divinely decided. Believe me, you all arrived exactly when I needed you most. I am forever grateful.

Table of Contents

1

Beginnings

Having fun with the Sacred
is having a divine time.

—Linda Luz Benvenue

Maya Angelou, the great American poet, penned the following: "A bird does not sing because it has an answer, it sings because it has a song." At first glance, it seemed that Ms. Angelou had it all wrong. As far as I was concerned a bird would sing if it had an answer. After all, isn't that life's search — struggling to find just the right answers? Who cares about the song? Well, my hat's off to you, Maya Angelou. It appears you discovered long before me that a bird's song expresses its oneness with the Great Bird of the Sky. Its warbles and chirps form its personal mantra as it flies freely in a cloud of knowingness out of which all answers flow. My life has been a search for my song. Little did I know that like the "bird," the melody was alive in me from the start. All I had to do was allow the notes to come together, open my mouth, and let the music begin.

Tuesday, November 17, 2004. "Mom, when are you going to write about the extraordinary things that have occurred in your life? People need to read your story."

A simple question asked by my daughter prompted me to sit down and try to explain some of the more unusual happenings that helped shaped my life. To the reader, I ask: Do you believe you should share with the public incidents in your life that may seem too absurd to be believable or too personal to be shared— even if such disclosures could impact another's life and be the springboard for change? Loving to bask in the realm of possibilities, my intention in writing this spiritual memoir is to relate honestly, humbly, and with no pretense, certain events that occurred in my life that I believe could make a difference in yours.

I popped into the world fortunately neither chirping nor with any answers to speak of. Like everyone else, I arrived with a blank slate waiting to be filled. It certainly didn't take long before my significant others had it teeming with the do's and don'ts expected of a Portuguese/Italian girl born in South Philadelphia, who at the age of five moved to the suburbs with her parents and baby brother, Manny.

If I had to describe me during the first ten years of my life, I'd say I was a skinny, blue-eyed, blonde, whose nature leaned more towards compliancy though not timidity, daring but not stupidity. I loved running races, roller skating, riding my bike, and most of all walking through the woods picking violets for my mom.

My favorite sanctuary was the woods behind our little house. I would often sit atop a hugh rock overlooking a vacant quarry mesmerized by the light beams streaming through the trees and dancing like diamonds atop the water. It was there I learned that when left alone with silence as your friend, the most wonderful dreams can be born. Even though the nuns at the school I attended told us that God was invisible and lived "somewhere up there," I believed the woods, being so beautiful, was heaven and that God was hiding somewhere waiting to be found. I recall walking through the bushes and brambles hoping I'd catch a glimpse of him.

One of the first things we learned in first grade was that we were created to know, love, and serve God. I figured my first question if I ran into him would be, "How am I supposed to serve you when I don't even know what you need?" As I figured it, if you can't see somebody how do you know what they want? It was a daunting dilemma that followed me through a good part of my life.

Around the time I was ten, I began making short visits to church during my lunch break at school. Since it was only a block or so away, I'd hurry and eat, then off I'd go to sit amongst the beautifully stained glass windows and finely chiseled statues of Our Lady and the Sacred Heart near the altar area. Kneeling in the empty, dark church — save for the brilliantly colored rays of sunlight shining through the prisms of the church windows — I'd begin my utterances of memorized prayers in a voice barely above a whisper. These prayers came more from my lips than my heart. It never dawned on me to talk to God like I would my friends. When you went to church, silence was the order of things. Although I found quiet more befitting my temperament, whenever my heart overflowed with feelings I couldn't verbally express, I'd simply bow my head and whisper another prayer from memory.

One day, however, as I was preparing to leave the church strong emotions poured from my heart and I heard myself say in a rather loud voice, "God, I really love you." I stood there for a few seconds shocked that I had spoken so boldly to the Lord. Did those words come from my lips? Nope. For the first time I knew I had heard my heart speak. Running back to school I felt lighthearted and absolutely exhilarated and with a secret in my heart — I had talked to God. The wonder of that hallowed moment left my heart billowing over with delight and my eyes moistened from the joy of it all.

What happened that lovely afternoon when I was ten was the beginning of the many dialogues I had with the Lord. I remember the day I decided to ask him straight out if he also loved me; after all, one-way communications leave you with a little longing. I sat in the pew with my head down — more out of fear than reverence — and waited. I don't know what I was expecting to hear. I literally held my breath hoping something would come across the air waves. But, silly me, nothing! I was after all young and assumed that if you believed with all your heart anything was possible. It would take quite a few years before I'd come to understand the ways in which God was seeking to manifest himself to me.

2

The Developing Years

The brave will always tackle
things they fear most
so not to be shackled.

—*Linda Luz Benvenue*

My teen years were uneventful except for the summer months when I worked at a Catholic nursing home for the elderly run by the Bon Secour Sisters. As an aide, my job was to attend to the female patients. Each day I'd bathe them, change their bed clothes and linens, and feed those unable to do so. How deeply touched I was by their gentleness and sincerity. In conversation, I found it absolutely amazing how honest they were in discussing with me their personal experiences, sharing not only what they had gained from life, but also of the distractions that had set them back. Their favorite question to me was, "Are you listening, Linda?" Yes, my friends to this day — some fifty-five years later — I'm still listening and remembering. I have not forgotten you.

One of the most disheartening things to deal with was the awareness that death was never far away. When I would finish my shift, I'd make it a point to say good-bye to all my little ladies never knowing whose bed would be empty the next day. When I would say, "See you in the morning, girls," they responded, "Hope so, Linda, hope so." We all understood the underlying sentiment in their heartfelt response.

When I graduated high school, I decided to become an x-ray technician and trained at a Catholic hospital in Darby, Pennsylvania. Those were fun years. I loved caring for the patients and met many wonderful health-care givers. After receiving my certification I decided to move on and find a job paying more than the thirty-five dollars every two weeks they offered me. A friend of mine told me of a position available in Center City, Philadelphia. I applied, got the job, and worked at the Medical Tower building for three years for a group of radiologists.

How I loved Philly! And why not? I was born just a few miles away and my grandparents still lived there. The best part of each day was my treasured lunch hour. I can't tell you all the stores and little shops I would hustle through in sixty minutes. Inevitably, I'd always find a "must have" before rushing back to work.

During that time, I was still living at home with my parents. My mode of transportation to and from was the train. Donned in a crisp uniform and wearing freshly polished white shoes, I'd hop on the train for the forty-minute trek to Philly where I would meander down Seventeenth Street stopping for coffee along the way. Those morning strolls were the best! The people I passed were so friendly, saying "good morning" and nodding. I'm convinced that what attracted them was my white uniform and what it meant. I was proud of my Nightingale garb. If a nun wore a habit, then that was mine. It was a constant reminder of the commitment I'd made when I worked at the nursing home. "Lord, lead me to where you want me to be and by your grace help me to heal hearts that are hurting." I call this my intention prayer and continue to embrace it daily. Having witnessed death often at the nursing home, I arrived at a point where I was ready to have the authentic desires of my heart sanctified and blessed by God. I felt that to be effective, my desires had to be expressed simply and in my own words. I believe that to offer and dedicate the desires of your heart to God is a good thing.

3

The White Hood Gang

Patience, so hard attained,
reminds me of chess;
so few know the game.

—Linda Luz Benvenue

Although I loved working in a radiologist's office, after several years I longed to utilize all my skills as an x-ray technician, which could only be done in a hospital setting. Plus, I really did miss working with the sickly. At that time, I had a good friend who worked for a private radiologist who had recently been appointed chief of radiology at a new Catholic hospital in Chester, Pennsylvania. I asked if she would speak to him on my behalf, which she did, and that started the ball rolling. I was interviewed and within one month found myself working in the bowels of Sacred Heart Hospital in the x-ray department, sandwiched between the emergency room and morgue.

The hospital was run by the Bernadine Sisters of the Order of St. Francis. What a caring group of women they were — down to earth and very inquisitive, especially about my weekend exploits and activities. Since I was the only technician in the department who was not a nun, they had a field day grilling me, especially on Monday mornings. "Linda, what did you do this weekend?" "Did you have a date?" "Where did you go?" And their most favorite of all, "Are you going to see him again?" Several of these women became my dearest friends. It was a beautiful time in my life.

Looking back, I can see the subtle movement of God's hand nudging me forward a little measure at a time, leading me to where I was to be and what I was to do next. All I had to do was pay heed to that persistent force and be ready to move — as they say, in a New York minute. Even though I could at times sense when something was about to unfold, I seldom had any idea what.

In the winter of 1959, I wasn't dating much because there wasn't anyone out there that I was interested in, so I'd spend my weekends going to dances with my friends and then in the summer we'd drive down to the Jersey shore. On weekdays, I worked very hard while enjoying my favorite thing—running up to the chapel whenever I had a chance to talk to God, just as I did in my school days. It was important that he knew all the patients who needed his help, so I'd spew out their names—like he didn't know already. Anyway, the nuns found it curious that I visited the chapel so often. In their minds, as I later found out, they thought since I wasn't dating much, I might be considering the religious life as a vocation. Actually, they weren't far off center because I did from time to time consider that possibility. However, I thought I also wanted to marry and have children. Such a dilemma.

One afternoon, the two nuns from x-ray cornered me and very seriously approached the subject. "Linda, have you ever considered the religious life as a vocation?" Looking at them curiously and wondering where that question came from, I said, "Why yes, Sisters, I have, but I think I'd also like to be a wife and mom. I'm just not sure yet." They both looked at me very seriously and then one said, "Linda, Sister and I would like to suggest that you make a novena to Saint Joseph to help you with your decision. In fact, we'll make it with you and if after that period you haven't met anyone then perhaps the religious life is your path."

For anyone not familiar with a Catholic novena it's a nine-day series of prayers or devotions offered for a particular intent. In this instance it would be offered to Saint Joseph for the purpose of assisting me with my decision. The prayers are said with reverence and great expectation. Since these nuns really loved me and were concerned with my future, the least I could do was go along with their suggestion. Besides, I loved the novena to Saint Joseph. As far as I was concerned it was a win-win situation, as I had everything to gain. My feeling was "no stone unturned; no prayer unheard."

On the eighth day of the novena, which was a Sunday, I went to visit a friend who was a patient at another hospital in the area. After speaking with him for about an hour, his doctor walked into the room and my friend introduced us. "Linda, I'd like you to meet Dr. John Blizzard." "Nice meeting you," I said, smiling. I was certainly impressed by the fact that this physician was visiting his patients on a Sunday. My friend informed me that Dr. Blizzard had just joined the staff at Sacred Heart Hospital. He followed that with, "Isn't that where you work, Linda?" He knew I did. That was thrown in for his doctor to pick up. Before I said anything, my eyes went to his left ring finger. Hmmm, no wedding band, I thought to myself—maybe he's single? Nah, can't be! Most doctors are married before they get out of medical school. However, I liked to think that he wasn't.

The three of us talked for quite a while. After he left my friend said, "I think my doctor was impressed with you, Linda, He never visited this long and he forgot to ask how I was doing." "R-e-a-l-l-y," I said, while thinking how I could manage running into him at the hospital where I worked. Hmm, could this be a happening?

The next morning while driving to work my thoughts were on how I was going to tell the good sisters — with only one novena day left — that I had met someone I found interesting and would like to get to know better. Had Saint Joseph answered my prayers? One thing was for sure, I wanted to date Dr. John Blizzard, but how would I get him to call me? How would I meet him again?

When I got to the hospital, I thought it best to tell my friends during our coffee break about my weekend find. I must say I really expected them to be disappointed, but on the contrary, they wanted to hear more and more about my encounter with the doctor. I told them all I knew, as well as the fact that I was very faithful in keeping my novena. As far as I was concerned you don't go ninety miles in a hundred-mile race and quit. With that I walked up to the chapel to conclude the last day of my novena to Saint Joseph.

When the two nuns returned from lunch that afternoon, the look on their faces was like that of little girls trying to hide a big secret. Since the department was a little slow they whisked me away to our favorite coffee spot. You had to see the scene! They were scurrying down the corridor with white habits flying about, rosary beads dancing in the air, and looking back to make sure no one saw where we were headed.

"Hey, what's going on? What are you two up to?"

"Sit down, Miss Luz, we want to talk to you."

"Miss Luz! Since when did I become Miss Luz?"

"Sit! Sit! Sit!"

"OK, Sisters, I'm sitting."

And then they started.

"Doctor Blizzard's not only on staff here, but he's one of our Sister's physicians. He arrives almost every day around two o'clock in the afternoon to see his patients on Second Medical. He and his buddy, Dr. Jack, share an office in town and both are on staff at two other hospitals, and no, he's isn't married. Anything else you'd like to know?"

"Would I? Where in heavens did you get all this information and have you figured out how I can get to meet him again?"

"Linda, we have an idea. Listen to this."

Well, let me tell you, my head was spinning when I heard the plan they had concocted. These two nuns were going to play medical "I spy" along with the rest of their cohorts on Second Medical.

They were out to make sure that Linda Luz met her doctor again. When I heard what they had put together, I thought they were all crazy. But taking no chances I walked up to the chapel and asked God to take part in the fun and, if possible, make it all happen. I prayed that the mission of the "white hood gang," as I called my little nuns, would be successful. Here was the plan.

At approximately 1:45 in the afternoon, a nun from Second Medical would keep watch over the parking lot checking for Doctor Blizzard's arrival. When his car was spotted, she'd call the x-ray department, letting the phone ring twice and then hang up. That was the clue — two rings and run! Up to the second floor I'd go, hanging around the nurse's station until the unsuspecting doctor appeared. Unfortunately, he never came around when expected. No one was quite sure where he disappeared to. Three weeks of running up and down became frustrating and I decided that playing cupid's game was a waste of time. But, oh no, not my friends; they came up with one more plan guaranteed to succeed. The "white hood gang" was brutal!

It was brought to the attention of my friends that Doctor Blizzard often read cardiograms at the heart station on Second Medical before he left the hospital. If you didn't see him going in that room you'd miss him completely. The heart station was located about fifty feet from the elevator that led down to where he would exit the hospital. When he was spotted leaving the heart station, I'd get the "ring and run" signal and off I'd go to the elevator, press the button to the second floor, get off, and stand there with my hand on the outside button so the door couldn't close. I can't tell you how many times I rode that thing. Then one day, there he was approaching the elevator and coming right towards me. There was no way he could avoid me. I looked at him and said, "Hi, going my way?" He smiled and I knew as we stepped into the elevator together I was on my way to having my first date with Doctor John Blizzard. Before he left, he had my phone number in his pocket. Yes! The plan of the "white hoods gang" had finally worked.

After a two-year courtship, John Blizzard and Linda Luz were married, becoming man and wife on September 16, 1961. Most of the nuns were there to witness the celebration. There was no way they were going to miss this event since they had orchestrated it from the very beginning—with the help of Saint Joseph, of course. After we were married, I continued working until an ongoing medical problem from my teens caused me to take a leave of absence.

Here I was twenty-four and still suffering with severe abdominal pains that would last for days. All I wanted to do was stay in bed until the discomfort passed. During that time, I'd pray hard for God to give me the "fix" I needed to go on just one minute more. That "fix" was his grace. I believe from my soul that "grace is something God gives us to stand what we cannot understand." I'm not sure who said that, but the truth of it is certainly undeniable. Although I can't explain it, I can certainly feel its movement inside of me. It's like a heightened awareness that the "something" I need to move forward is there. All I have to do is trust in its power and begin to take the next step.

Through the years my parents took me to several doctors but none could find the cause for the pain. After a while I began to sense that everyone thought it was all imaginary. After all, if a cause can't be found then the problem doesn't exist. Such was the mentality back in the sixties. For fear my husband would think the same, I never told him about my physical dilemma until after we were married a month. Well, John Blizzard, an exceptional physician, believed me and suggested I see his good friend, a well known gynecologist in the area. I did and within a week I was admitted for surgery in the very same hospital where I worked.

Following the procedure both the surgeon and my husband came to my room to discuss the findings.With great sensitivity and concern they explained that a dozen or more small tumors had to be removed from my abdominal and pelvic area. Although benign, they explained they were the result of an advanced condition called endometriosis. Trying to understand what they were saying was impossible. I was only able to digest the fact that this so-called "condition" made it difficult, if not impossible, to conceive. I was devastated. All those years of severe pain seemed absolutely futile and served no purpose whatsoever. Don't think I didn't pass that on to the Lord.

Being twenty-four, it was recommended that I consider going on hormonal therapy as a course of treatment. After speaking with my gynecologist, that's exactly what I did. I must say, although I was saddened by the fact that pregnancy might escape me, I was happy to be relieved of the awful pain and to put to rest the idea that it was all in my noggin. I can remember beginning and ending many a day with the words, "Thank you, God." Whatever's in store for me in the future I accept and stand by your grace." I meant that with all my heart, even though I had no idea what the future would bring.

The events that occurred during the next five years of my life continue to have an impact on me even today. Sadly, the prescribed mode of hormonal treatment I was on was unsuccessful and by the time I was twenty-nine, I had undergone three more surgeries, including a total hysterectomy. Here I was facing the onset of menopause at a young age with no possibility of ever conceiving a child. Even though the idea of becoming pregnant was absurd, I'd often sit and wonder what it would be like to have a baby growing in my tummy and feeling its movement. I wanted to give life. I wanted to be a mom. Interestingly, I'm not so sure John felt the same. Although we talked about it, he seemed rather complacent about the idea. It was almost as if it didn't matter to him one way or the other. He understood my needs to a degree, but that's as far as it went.

How I envied my sister-in-law, Betty Cepis, my husband's sister. She and her husband, John, had already brought into the world nine of their thirteen children. Actually, I don't think I ever saw her un-pregnant! Yes, life is beautiful, but there are times when it can leave you traumatized asking, "How can this be?" After the hysterectomy I had time to try to make sense of the events that had occurred in my life. I've always said that life is a mystery that unfolds in time—God's time. But this time it was my time to vent.

For months I'd chatter away about this or that hoping to come up with a sense of purpose for my existence. When I finally stopped and began listening, the awareness came that everything I desired and hoped for was already laid out as a reality before me just waiting to be discovered. All I had to do was walk towards it and it would make itself known. Without any doubt I was being asked to implicitly trust in a power I still couldn't see, yet said I believed in. I found this, to say the least, a bit challenging and more unnerving than ever. I felt like I was back in the woods still searching for God. It was the same old question. Did I have that kind of trust willing to believe in a love I couldn't see? It's like the story of the man falling off the top of a mountain and as he's going down grabs onto a limb jutting out from the rock and starts crying out to God for help. Hearing his plea, God asks the man some questions.

"Do you love me?"

"Lord, you know I love You"

"But, do you trust me?"

"Yes, Lord, you know I trust you."

"Well, then let go."

Frightened for his life the man looks up and asks rather sheepishly, "Anybody else up there?" I'm sure that man *thought* he trusted. But thoughts can be deceiving. I've found that God's way of teaching us about ourselves is to offer each one of us the opportunity to meet face to face the person we think we are, or, are not. It's the behavior we exhibit daily, as we go through life's paces facing our personal challenges, that reflects the authenticity of the beliefs we hold dear. To know the truth of us is to hold life's mirror to our face and glimpse the accuracy of our beliefs. In this way we truly come to know ourselves.

4

A Time for Miracles

Watch closely what you do,
for always watching others
is little use to you.

—Linda Luz Benvenue

In January, 1967, one year after my hysterectomy, I awoke with the proverbial light bulb going off in my head. Since we both wanted children, why not adopt? After tossing the idea around in my mind for a few days, I approached John, and he agreed it would be OK if that's what I wanted. What I wanted? I thought to myself. What about you? John was never great at expressing his true feelings. Actually, he was best at concealing them. His broad smile was the facade behind which he hid his personal fears and disappointments, and that facade was impenetrable even to me. He was a brilliant, caring endocrinologist who excelled in his profession, yet as his wife and friend, I was never really sure I had reached the heart of the man. However, knowing how much he loved his nieces and nephews, I decided it was time to love a child of our own.

My chatter with God the next several days was simple and direct. I asked for his grace and guidance to make this all come to fruition. Within several weeks, we were led to two attorneys who dealt with adoptions. The first gentleman told us it would take about four months before he might have a child ready for adoption. The other said that, at that time, no child was available. Taking no chance, we asked each to place us on their waiting list. John and I were prepared to wait the year or more it normally took to adopt an infant.

On March 7, 1967, just two months after visiting the two attorneys, the phone rang and I heard someone say on the other end, "Hello, Linda, this is Jim, your attorney. I called to ask a question. How would you like a baby boy?"

I held my breath and couldn't say a word. Finally, he questioned if I was still there. "Oh yes of course, I'm still here!" Figuring it would be months before the baby's birth. I asked, "When will he be born?"

"How about eleven o'clock this morning?" he replied.

"What! Oh, my sweet Jesus, I can't believe this is happening! Yes! Yes! I'm ready for our son," I cried out.

With tears dripping down my face I heard him say, "Congratulations, Linda, You and John are now the parents of a beautiful little baby boy weighing in at seven pounds, two ounces."

My heart was bursting! As soon as I got off the phone I called my husband at the hospital telling him the good news. We were both giddy from all the excitement, and I was relieved to hear his response to the great news. Hanging up the phone, I thanked God and immediately knew he had been listening to my chatter all along.

From that day forward my life changed dramatically. We were advised by our attorney that he himself would be delivering the baby to our doorstep in two days. Two days! Yikes! Where do I start? After all, I wasn't prepared for the arrival of a baby so soon. I hadn't purchased a thing — no furniture, baby clothes, bottles, or diapers. Speaking of diapers, I wasn't even sure how to change one. Help! Somebody?

How great are family and friends at such a time. My mom and dad were ecstatic, as were Betty and her husband, John. Aunts and uncles pitched in to give advice on the "how to" of caring for a helpless little tyke just three days old and about to arrive at our home. As far as naming the little guy, when John asked what I thought would be a good name for the baby, I looked at him and said, "Why John Joseph Blizzard, Jr., of course." His smile reflected his pleasure.

When the doorbell rang my heart stopped. As I readied myself to open the door, I thought, here we go — instant motherhood! With the door fully opened, I immediately caught glimpse of a little bundle wrapped in a blue blanket and cradled in the arms of our attorney. His secretary stood behind him smiling, anticipating our joy. As I welcomed them my eyes never drifted from what he was holding in his arms. With few words exchanged and arms extended he handed me our son.

How absolutely deafening the pounding of the heart can be when a miracle is near. Caught up in my own little world, I continued staring at the blanket covering his face until I heard my husband say, "Lindy, lift the blanket, I want to see our son." No longer transfixed, I slowly rolled it back to discover the most beautiful face I ever saw, so perfect, so round, and with eyes open and lovingly fixed on me. As I looked at him, tears from my eyes fell onto his little cheeks. I buried my head next to his and said, "Straight from heaven to your new home. We welcome you John Joseph Blizzard, Jr." Jubilant applause and shouts of welcome came from family members there to witness this blessed event. My husband was beaming. "What a handsome boy," he said, smiling. The days and weeks that followed were the beginning of a new chapter for both of us. I couldn't help but think what a difference a single day can really make.

5
A Background Check

Man's mind carried too far
stops him from seeing
most things as they are.

—*Linda Luz Benvenue*

During the first six years of our marriage, before our son's arrival, John and I had a problem with compatibility. In 1962, we separated after living together for only five months. With John spending most of his time outside the home it was strenuous on our marriage. While I was twenty-four, looking for a loving partner and companion, he was thirty-five, accustomed to living in a world of his own that was difficult for me to penetrate. Interestingly, when working at the hospital, he was totally different. He held his private life in check and bedazzled everyone with his charm, intelligence, and smile. But once at home, he retreated into his private world where it became obvious I didn't have a place. He'd spend hours in the bedroom reading all kinds of magazines. In any given day we barely spent more than an hour together.

I remember our first Christmas. After opening his gifts, John went directly to the bedroom and read *Time* magazine while I sat alone in front of the tree opening presents and feeling physically and emotionally abandoned. I spent most of the day crying my heart out and wishing I was home with my parents and brother, who I knew were enjoying the day that I loved most in the year.

As a newlywed, I found it difficult to work through the isolation and problems his indifference caused. Did I love him? Yes, very much. But love has its own needs and when ignored assumes an altered posture. Although we discussed the problem, I wasn't one to push the envelope for fear he'd walk away saying, as usual, I was immature and naive. Immature? I don't think so. Naive? Yes, that I admit. If it's childlike to want to receive and give love and trust in its transforming power, then may I always retain such innocence. It wasn't long before I realized it was time to move on.

After the separation, I lived with my parents while continuing to work at the hospital. I can't tell you how difficult that was, especially since the nuns were genuinely affected by the situation. As match-makers the "white hood gang" really tried bringing us together by letting me know how awfully sad Doctor John looked, and I didn't look much better. I guess in time their strategy worked. Several months later, I returned to the marriage hoping to salvage a relationship I truly believed was crafted by God. Did it work? I'm afraid not. In 1964, after being separated yet another time, I divorced my husband and went off to live in Center City, Philadelphia determined to find a new life.

Being familiar with the city and knowing my way around was great. I rented a small efficiency near Rittenhouse Square close to where I worked as a receptionist. I loved my job and with lots of friends around, I was never alone. As far as dating, I seldom did. Strangely I still felt a sense of commitment to my ex-husband, John. Why? I'm not quite sure, but believed it to be because I knew although divorced by the state we were still husband and wife in the eyes of the Catholic Church.

About a year or so into my new life, I was introduced to a gentleman, who, like John, was a bit older than me. After dating for eight months, he proposed, and I accepted. One day as I was strolling through the square on my way to a nearby church — as usual to talk to God about the pending wedding — I suddenly caught sight of John Blizzard standing no more than forty feet to my right. Knowing he hadn't seen me, I stepped up my pace trying to disappear into the crowd. Although we were divorced for almost a year, John would call on occasion to ask how I was doing and if I'd like to go to dinner. Although I was polite in refusing the invitation, I was left wondering why he hadn't shown me such attention while we were married. I knew he wanted me to come back, but that could never be. He had no idea I was planning to marry someone else.

When I finally arrived at the church, I sat in the pew trying to calm myself. Seeing John in the square had unnerved me. It was time to tell him about my pending marriage. As I looked around the church I became aware that the silence that always brought me joy now brought sadness. I sat there for about ten minutes staring into holy space. Not a word or salutation could I offer my God. Confounded by my muteness, I decided to leave. As I was halfway down the aisle to exit the church, I heard someone speaking in a rather loud voice saying, "GO BACK, LINDA! GO BACK!"

Who said that? I thought as I looked around seeing no one. Certain of what I heard I became a bit frightened and began moving quickly towards the door when the words, "GO BACK, LINDA! GO BACK began to resonate from a cavernous place within myself. Tripping out the exit door, I began yelling, "No! No! It's my life, and I will never go back to John Blizzard!" I left that church running at a pretty good clip back to my apartment where I sat for hours in shock and frightened, still trying to make sense of what had just happened. I felt certain that seeing John that day triggered something inside of me. Falling asleep that night, I thought how after all these years God had finally communicated with me and I didn't like what he had to say.

About a month after the incident, I was given a bridal shower by my fiancé's family, even though we hadn't set a wedding date. When the time came to open the gifts, I was handed one to unwrap. As I opened the box I suddenly felt as though I was being whisked away to another place. Everything became absolutely still. People's faces blurred and the noise that once filled the room faded. Unaware I was teetering back and forth, my mom grabbed hold of my arm to steady me and asked if I was OK. Hearing her call out to me, it felt as if I was being swept back from another dimension into the present. Everyone kept asking, "What's wrong? Are you all right, Linda?" When I sat down and found my calm I said the excitement of the shower probably made me feel a bit lightheaded and queasy. How could I tell them that what had actually happened was so profound I wasn't able to talk about it with anyone?

At the moment I opened the first gift, I heard

these words gush from my core and echo through every cell of my body, "THIS CANNOT BE! YOU'VE BEEN THROUGH THIS ONCE BEFORE." There was no sensing these words. I heard them loud and clear and recognized the voice. It was the same as I the one I heard in the church just a month before. Although everyone that afternoon was very gracious and concerned, I seemed to be in another place observing myself rather sadly. When I went home that night all I could say was "Why, God, why?" It didn't take long before I knew what had to be done. Three days later, I broke my engagement. My fiancé was devastated and asked that I give it more time. I told him it was no use. Time was not the problem.

I never prayed as hard as I did during the following week. I talked and talked to God but knew where he wanted me. The only thing left to do was to call John and tell him I was coming back. He knew that wasn't what I really wanted to do, but he was happy regardless. His Lindy was coming home — again. The Hound of Heaven had won, but I was feeling no joy whatsoever. I returned to John on June 1, 1966.

Going back to a place one doesn't want to be is very difficult — at least it was for me. Not working and with time on my hands, I'd sit day after day in the rocker staring out the window. Knowing all the symptoms of depression, John asked if I'd like to see a professional. Hearing him say that, I thought to myself, *Doesn't he know why I'm depressed? I don't want to be here! It's that simple.* Finally in July I agreed to see one of his colleagues who'd pick my brain looking for causes from the past that were negatively affecting my future. I must say, I was grateful to let it all hang out. I told the doctor what he wanted to know, especially my reason for being depressed. I held nothing back. After three months of weekly meetings, this doctor leaned over his desk and said, "Linda, I don't think your marriage to John can go the distance. You are both so totally different. It's my medical and professional opinion that if you stay together you'll end up killing each other in the end." Since this man was a personal friend of my husband's, I was stunned to put it mildly by his rather subjective evaluation of our situation — even if it was what I wanted to hear. Leaving his office that day in October I looked back, said good-bye, and knew I'd never be seeing him again. I never did.

After giving me his prognosis of what might happen if I stayed with John, something clicked inside my head. Who was he to tell me what lay in my future or for that matter what I could or could not do? As far as I was concerned, a power higher than his wanted John and me together. Walking out that door and onto the elevator, I challenged myself to find the reason why. I was left to trust implicitly in the Providence of an invisible force directing my life. Throughout the years I often said to God, "Please, don't let me roam too far off course; you know how bad my sense of direction is." As I saw it, he took me quite seriously.

During the fall of 1966 and feeling much better about the possibility of remarrying John, I realized that if I wanted to spend more time with him then perhaps I could work with him. It's the same old story; if the mountain won't come to you then you go to the mountain. Since there wasn't a nurse or receptionist at his local office, John thought it would be great if we worked together on the three nights he held hours. *This could be a good thing,* I thought to myself. Three days later, the doctor and his new assistant headed off to help and heal the sick.

My first impression of his office was "Oh my God! What did I let myself in for?" I was dismayed at the mess I found. Files were strewn in piles on the floor, many with checks or cash inside. The waiting room was dreary with only a small ceiling lamp lit, and the walls were barren with not one diploma hanging. Immediately, I sized the place up and knew what had to be done. Driving home, I rather nonchalantly asked John if I could spruce the office up a bit. He said exactly what I wanted to hear, "Sure, Lindy, anything you want to do is fine with me." Within a few weeks the office was completely transformed. It looked so sunny and bright with almost everything new including rugs, furniture, medical equipment, and filing cabinets. I also made sure his medical diplomas were hung on the walls around the office. John taught me how to take blood pressure, do electrocardiograms, as well as simple blood and urine tests. I also did all the billing, which previously had been done by an agency. I can honestly say I was beginning to feel happy for the first time in a long time, and it was beginning to show.

Before continuing, I have to say when I worked at the office, I never expected to see what my eyes beheld and my ears heard. The patients absolutely loved Dr. John Blizzard. To them he was a home-grown savior who never forgot his beginnings and opened an office amongst those he had once lived among. I heard stories of how he saved patients' lives by visiting them at home when no other doctor would. They'd say to me, "Mrs. Blizzard, the Doc was the only who'd come, and he only charged eight dollars for the visit. I thought to myself, *Hmmm, well that's about to change.*

It didn't take long for me to realize how self-centered I had previously been. Here was a man who got out of bed at five-thirty every morning so he could be at the hospital by seven to start rounds. Arriving home a little after five in the evening, he'd eat his dinner quickly so he could be at his local office by six p.m. I began to ask myself, *Who is this man?* He had needed my help all along but being so absorbed in satisfying my own needs, I neglected his. On the other hand, did pride keep him from approaching me when he knew he definitely needed someone to assist him? Well, that's yesterday's late news. I just want to say, I worked alongside John Blizzard for many years thereafter, happily.

January, 1967. Having lived together for eight months since my return the previous June, John and I were married in a civil ceremony in Wilmington, Delaware by the mayor. There was no pomp, no hoopla, just two people aware that their paths were meant to crystallize — at this place in time.

6

Back to Mothering

One's hope is best sustained
by seeking the truth
from those who have gained.

—Linda Luz Benvenue

It was three months after John and I remarried that our son, John Joseph Jr., came into our lives.

Life was good and I certainly loved being a mom. John was as busy as ever and I continued working with him at the office three nights a week. Thankfully, my parents offered to baby sit, for which I was very grateful. I must say I thought repeatedly of how much I would have missed if God had not been so persistent in pointing the way, and if I hadn't challenged myself to listen and follow his prompting. Soon I was to learn the implications of saying "yes" to God and "no" to my selfish inclinations.

June 17, 1967. I was sitting in the kitchen enjoying a wonderful cup of morning coffee when the phone rang. Thinking it was my husband I said, "Hi, Hon, what's up?" The voice on the other end was certainly not John's. Feeling somewhat embarrassed, I apologized and started laughing.

He immediately introduced himself and said, "Hi, Linda, this is Paul, your attorney."

"Oh hi, how are you?"

"I'm fine, but I'm sorry it took so long to get back to you."

"For what, may I ask?"

"For the baby, Linda."

"What baby, Paul?"

"Don't you remember about six months ago you and your husband came to see me about adopting a child and at the time I didn't have a client placing one for adoption?" I wasn't sure what I was hearing. Then the proverbial pin could have dropped when I heard him ask, "You and John are still interested in adopting a child, right?"

"Oh, you haven't heard, Paul; we already have a son who's now three months old."

"No, I had no idea. Congratulations!"

Before he could finish his sentence I was already thinking to myself, *Lord, have you chosen another child for us to love and raise? Can we do it? Can I take care of two infants only three months apart at the same time?* Putting a hold on my thoughts, I asked our attorney to please give me a few moments while I called John to tell him of the unbelievable opportunity that had fallen from heaven into our laps. John was speechless but very excited when he heard he would be a dad for a second time. When he asked if he had a son or daughter, I said, "I don't know. I never asked." We both started laughing. We had indeed come a long way.

Within several minutes, I was back on the phone with our attorney telling him we definitely wanted our new baby. He was delighted and said the words I had just heard three months prior. "Congratulations, Linda, you are the mom of a fine-looking baby boy born this morning." I was happy, grateful, and excited all at the same time. I immediately called John again and relayed the good news.

"Honey, you're not going to believe this."

"I can believe anything you tell me, Lindy."

"Well, John, you just had a baby boy this morning."

"Oh my goodness, who would have thought?"

"You're right and who would've thought we have to pick him up in three days from the hospital where he was born?"

"Wow!" was all John could say, trying to keep his

composure as he said good-bye. As I turned to put the phone down, I thought to myself, *Here we go again, barely enough time to put things in order before the arrival of our son.* Thank God, I had a little practice by then.

There was a sense of wonder that seemed to surround this joyous happening. I couldn't believe we would walk into the hospital empty-handed and walk out with our son. Yes! It was unbelievable and about to happen. More of God's plan for us was unfolding by the minute.

Our baby boy who we named Jeffrey Joseph, was born at the same hospital where I had worked and where John was still on staff. We knew everyone there and I was anxious to see my friends, "the white hood gang," again.

When we arrived at the hospital, we were told to go directly to the maternity floor, where we were asked if we would like to dress our son in his going-home outfit Amid the shrieks of babies crying in the nursery and the ooh's and aah's of proud family members, I fell silent as tears began sweeping across my eyes. The good nun knew my answer and brought us to a small dressing table where we awaited the arrival of our Jeffrey. Within minutes, Sister returned with six other nuns in tow and an absolutely beautiful little baby, half-naked, and tucked securely in her arms. Handing our son to me, she said, "Linda, I believe this little package was delivered for you and Doctor John. God has chosen well. Bless you both."

With his body snuggled in my arms, I leaned over and began planting kisses on his forehead. When I handed our baby to John all the nuns were beaming with a slight mist covering their eyes. It wasn't long before our little guy let out some honest to goodness "I'm starving" cries.

After John and I finished dressing him, one of the nuns returned and said "I think I hear a hungry baby wanting to be fed". Handing me the bottle she said, "After you feed you son, Linda, the Sisters would like you and Doctor to join us in the chapel to offer prayers of thanksgiving to the Holy Family, if that's OK with both of you." Since John and I were both Catholic and loved many of the traditions of the church, we told her we'd be honored to join them.

With our baby well fed, dressed and bundled, we made our way down to the chapel. What I saw as we entered the chapel took my breath away. There directly ahead, kneeling reverently and singing softly as only these loving women can do, were about twenty nuns from throughout the hospital who had gathered to thank and praise God for our miracle. It was overwhelming to think that these gracious ladies who loved my husband and me were the catalyst for initially helping to bring John and me together. Taking our seats, the sisters began the service by offering prayers of praise and thanksgiving and singing hymns to Mother Mary befitting the occasion — especially, the "Ave Maria." Before the conclusion of the intimate service they asked if we would approach the altar rail to offer our own personal prayers to God.

Kneeling at the altar with our baby in my arms, I lifted him slightly and said, "Father, I offer you our child. Anoint his little life so he is able to know and love you as we have. As temporary care-givers placed in his life for reasons known only by you, help John and me to humbly accept this honor. We pray, Amen." Returning to our pew the nuns concluded the touching ceremony by singing my favorite hymn to Mary, the "Hail, Holy Queen."

Walking out of the hospital, we both felt like we were walking on a cloud. I was thrilled to hear a woman say as we got onto the elevator to go to our car, "Let's make room for the new baby and its parents.Is it a boy or girl?"

"A boy," I told her.

"Is this your first?"

"Oh no, we have another son at home."

"Ah, what a nice family you have."

"Yes, we sure do," I said, thanking her.

John was grinning and beaming as usual. Riding home I kept saying to myself, "Thank you, God, thank you." All that kept going through my head was thinking that in the past six months, I became a wife — again — and a mom to newborns not once, but twice. Holy Cow!

7

Who Would Believe?

Find glory in no deed,
but thank the heart
that planted the seed.

—Linda Luz Benvenue

Yes indeed, we had a wonderful family life that kept me busy, very busy, actually. With a new infant and a three-month-old to care for my days and nights were packed with plenty to do. I have to interject something here that's quite funny. When the boys got a little older strangers would ask if they were twins, and I'd jokingly reply, "Yes, three months apart."

Now, try to respond to that! The look on their faces was unbelievable! Jay Jay, as we called our first son, and Jeff didn't look at all alike. Jay Jay was fair with chestnut hair and the warmest brown eyes you ever saw on a face, while Jeff was ruddier with hair the color of the sun — a real towhead with piercing blue eyes. I called them back then my Prince and Nordic god and so they are to me today.

After Jeff's arrival, my husband asked if I wanted to stop working at his office in the evenings. I thought about it and decided that although the boys kept me busy, I still needed time for my husband. Besides, I loved the patients and would really miss them. John was pleased with my decision and suggested that we hire a qualified person to not only baby-sit three nights a week but also help me with the house chores during the day. Enter Virginia Morgan, another of God's great gifts just waiting in the wings for us. I can't tell you what she came to mean to my whole family. We all adored her, especially the children. She'd walk around the house singing and laughing in only the way that she could. How I depended on her expertise as a mom herself when my kids got sick. Although my husband was a physician, he wasn't a pediatrician and I needed someone with practical experience and that was Gin, as we called her. Besides, having a doctor in the house is the same as being married to a shoemaker. There were never any med samples around when you needed them.

Through the years, Gin and I became very close. We were definitely one in spirit spending time talking about life and trying to understand our purpose in it. Being very spiritual, she used the gift of her angelic voice to express her sentiments to the Lord. To this day, some forty years later, we continue to love her dearly. In fact, ask any of my kids who is Mom number two and they'll tell you right off — why Gin, of course. She and I still keep in touch.

You'd think by now and being so busy, I would've lost a bit of my selfish ways. Nope! I discovered another moniker to add to the list — ungrateful. Let me tell you why. After Jeff's arrival whenever I saw a pregnant woman I'd get a little down at the mouth because I couldn't bear a child of my own. I'd stare at their bellies and think to myself, *Do they know how lucky they are?* When I went to my gynecologist for a checkup, I both loved and hated it. Loved it because I would talk to the moms-to-be about how they were feeling and did they want a boy or a girl, etc. I hated it because I knew I could never be one of them. If that's not being ungrateful then tell me, what is? After all, I had two wonderful, healthy boys.

Whenever I prayed, although I did tell God how grateful I was for my sons, I'd throw in the fact that I felt a bit left out in having missed the whole pregnancy experience. My tune was always the same as I'd sit rubbing my belly lamenting over and over, "All I ever wanted was to know what it's like, that's all."

As I've stated I've never had a problem talking to God about my feelings, good or bad. He knows how I feel, so what's to hide? Besides, I never feel better than when I let go of my disappointments or false hopes. Since I know that God and I share an intimacy that demands absolute honesty, I trust in his love and I know he responds to my truthfulness.

As mentioned early on when I'm talking to God I'm praying to him. To always read formalized prayers written by someone else I'd say is a bit like cheating. I sense that God wants to hear what comes from our hearts no matter how simple or stupid we think it may sound. To me the simplest words rising from the heart make the greatest prayer. Sometimes, I get so caught up in the sentiments of a modest and simple "I love you," it takes my breath away and I seldom can say more. What more is there? At other times just reflecting on those words in silence makes me feel my heart will explode with love. Can anything be better than that?

Formalized prayers are extremely important and very appropriate. In community they keep people focused on why they have gathered. When said with heart, the Our Father, the beautiful rosary prayers, and those said to the saints, can raise the mind to heaven leaving one desiring a greater closeness with the Divine. All prayers rise to heaven. I just happen to think those that rise from the heart are more special. It's like sending cards to those we love. We can either buy a card with no verse inside allowing us to express what we genuinely feel or we can buy an all inclusive card that demands simply a signature. It's our choice. Whatever method one chooses to "talk" to God, hopefully it leads to surrender. Surrender is the ultimate prayer of unity. It's the joyous awareness that we are *one with the All That Is living within you and me.*

February, 1968. When the boys were almost a year old, I developed a problem that required a minor surgical procedure. Since I would have to be hospitalized for several days, John and I thought it best to have the procedure done when the weather was a bit warmer in the spring. This way, my parents, who would be sleeping over at night, could help Gin take care of the boys during the day, I spoke with my surgeon and arrangements were made for me to be admitted to the hospital that coming May.

May 17, 1968. During that particular afternoon, John called to say he wouldn't be home for dinner. Something had come up and he'd meet me at the office at six p.m. After feeding the boys, I left them with Gin and headed off to work alone. Patients began arriving on time but John hadn't. By six-thirty, the waiting room was packed and I was getting concerned. Finally, he walked into the office, apologized to the patients, looked at me and said, "Hi, Lindy, call Sister Martha at the hospital, she wants to talk to you." Before I had a chance to ask him why, he had whisked his first patient into his office.

After things settled down a bit, I decided to call my friend. I had a pretty good idea what she wanted. She was a knitter and when she'd run out of her favorite yarn I'd take her to town for more.

I called her at the hospital and said, "Hey, what's up? John said for me to call you. Do you want to go shopping for more yarn, Sister?"

"No, I don't think so, Linda."

"Then what can I do for you?"

"I think it's more like what I can do for you, my dear."

"Well, what you can do for me right now is to tell me what this call's all about. John was almost an hour late and we're really backed up in the office."

"Yes, I'm sure you are and I'm sorry, but Doctor John was here at the hospital for quite a while this afternoon."

"Aha! I wondered where he was," I said. "Why was he there so long, Sister?"

"There was something I needed to ask him before I discussed it with you, Linda."

"And pray tell what might that be, Sister?"

What that nun proceeded to tell me left me visibly shaking.

"Linda, we have a beautiful baby girl born yesterday that I believe has your name written all over her face and she's up for adoption. How would you like to be her mommy?"

In a rather shaky voice I asked her, "What did you say, Sister?"

"It's true, Linda, that's why Doctor John was here today. We needed to know if you were up to adding yet another baby to your family in less than eleven months."

"And what did he say, Sister?"

His exact words were, "My Lindy can do anything, but please Sister ask her yourself, she's at the office. Better yet, I'll have her call you as soon as I get there." She paused for a moment.

"Well, my dear Linda, what do you have to say?"

"Oh my goodness, Sister, I never thought I'd have a little girl. I've waited a long time for this to happen. Yes, I'm ready. When can I bring her home?"

"She'll be ready for you and your husband in several days."

Putting down the phone, I put my head on the desk and let the tears roll.

After composing myself, I started running back to the consultation room to tell John I had spoken to Sister when all of a sudden I stopped dead in my tracks. Oh dear Jesus, it's not possible. There's no way! How can it be that I'm going to have surgery in two days at the very same hospital where my little girl was just born? Caught up in some mystical bubble of awe and wonder, I went down on my knees trying to fathom what was about to happen. Weeks ago when my surgeon's office called to set a date for my surgery, I picked May 19 out of a hat thinking it was as good as any other day. Why did I choose May and why the nineteenth? I have no idea. Was this a coincidence or a major medical miracle about to take place? How was it possible to be admitted as a patient for surgery and go home with a baby? Unable to find words to express what I was feeling, I simply let myself be enveloped by the presence off the Divine sweeping through me. At that moment God and I were communing in absolute silence. No expression of gratitude was needed. He knew how I felt.

When John came out of the consultation room, I looked at him affectionately saying, "I told Sister, yes!" He nodded, smiled, and in that moment I knew that none of what had or was about to happen could if I hadn't followed God's promptings — rather reluctantly, I might add — and remarried this man sixteen months prior. Life had been slowly teaching me that doing what you don't want to do may be the very best thing to do. I certainly was proof of that.

On the morning I was to be admitted to the hospital, I kissed and hugged our boys telling them Daddy and I were going to bring home a new baby sister. Driving to the hospital we were both somewhat pensive. Arriving, we walked to the admissions office where we were pulled aside by two of my friends from the "white hood gang" who took us to a small room down the hall. There they informed us that only a handful of nuns knew what was about to transpire with our soon-to-be baby. They asked that we say nothing to anyone since confidentiality was most important. Giving our word, we were escorted back to admissions. What a freeze-frame moment that was! I've noticed that whenever nuns get excited they move around so quickly it's hard keeping up with them. These two were going at such a hardy clip down and around the halls they reminded me of Jake and Elwood from the movie "The Blues Brothers," who believed they were on a "mission from God." Ditto for the "white hoods." Depositing us safely at admissions, they said "good-bye" and told me they'd be seeing me later.

The nun in charge of admissions was a good friend but knew nothing about the baby. As far as she was concerned, I was there to have surgery the following morning. After signing the necessary papers she looked at me rather painfully and said, "Linda, I'm sorry to have to tell you this but we are bed poor at this time. Both the medical and surgical floors are bursting at the seams. Unfortunately, the only bed available is on maternity. But I promise as soon as a bed becomes available on surgical I'll have you switched." Without a moment's hesitation I spewed out, "Oh no, Sister, don't! I'm only going to be here a few days so it's really not a problem. Please, I'll be fine." When I worked at the hospital this very same nun often heard me talking about having a baby of my own there one day. Little did she know the time had arrived.

Sister escorted us to maternity. Getting off the elevator I heard little cries coming from the nursery and wondered if one of them belonged to my little girl. When we got to the nurse's station, Sister hugged me and wished me luck with my surgery. The nun in charge of maternity, Sister Matilda, welcomed us and then brought us to my room. When we were inside she closed the door and said she needed to speak with us. She told us that our baby's biological mother hadn't been discharged yet, and would I please not leave the room since she might be walking the hall. I told her not to worry, I would stay put. With that she opened the door and with her index finger to her lips said in a whisper, "Linda, look under your mattress when you get a chance." Winking at me with a grin on her face she quickly left. *Hmm,* I thought to myself, *this is all very mysterious.* Slipping my hand under the mattress I pulled out a medal of the Blessed Mother, a small pink baby rattle, and a beautifully knitted baby's cap — pink, of course. The moment was surreal. God and the good Sisters had thought of everything. All my husband and I could do was look at each other in amazement.

When John left I tried to settle in a bit but was overcome with excitement. I so wanted to visit the nursery. Knowing I gave my word, I decided to lie on the bed and let my mind roam freely. I knew I was watching a miracle happen! It was as if I was being guided step by step to the top of a special mountain and asked to look at the magnificent vista surrounding me. As I did, I was made aware it was God's mountain. Reflecting on that, I had a sense that *yes, it is God's mountain, but he created it for me and we are sharing it together.*

I must have dozed off when I heard a knock at my door. It was my surgeon stopping by to go over my surgery in the morning. Good grief! I had almost forgotten about that simple matter–which it really was. It was a minor urological procedure that would take no more than thirty minutes, I was told. After going through the do's and don'ts he wished me well, and said he was sure I'd breeze right through it. How I wanted to say, "I know that, after all there's a little baby waiting for me to take her home and I'm not about to disappoint her."

About six o'clock in the evening, Sister Matilda popped in briefly to take my vitals. She spruced up my bed and gave me a pre-op prep, which I drank down. Before she left she asked if she could stop by later in the evening for another chat. I told her that wouldn't be a problem since I wasn't going anywhere. Then out the door she scooted to help someone else.

I don't remember the exact time but an hour or so after visiting hours, I began to feel somewhat queasy in my stomach. Thinking it was probably a reaction to the day's events, I tried ignoring it but soon was feeling discomfort all over my abdomen. I thought of calling for the nurse but didn't want to seem like a baby. Within a half hour I was doubled up in the lounge chair with so much pain I couldn't even call out for the nurse or reach the buzzer by my bed. All I could do was toss and turn in that chair while holding my tummy trying to relieve the awful cramping. My moans and groans were getting louder and louder and I thought I was going to throw up all over myself. I remember looking up at a cross hanging behind the bed and with a trembling, frightened voice beseeched God saying, "Please, Father, help me! I can't take this pain anymore" By now I was in an absolute sweat, tears were running all over me, and my gown was sopping wet. Trying to get out of the chair to reach the buzzer and page the nurse, I felt my legs starting to give way under me. Holding on to a corner of the bed I let out a loud moan and began sobbing uncontrollably when all of a sudden I heard this deep voice blare out from somewhere inside of me, "WELL, YOU WANTED TO KNOW WHAT IT WAS LIKE!"

Startled, frightened, and still shaking with pain I knew there was no denying that voice. I'd heard it before and as before it was loud and very clear. Sitting on the bed, still holding my tummy, I cried, "Yes, Father, I did. But did you have to go this far? I'm feeling really awful." Just about then Sister Matilda walked into my room, looked at me, and said, "My goodness sounds like somebody in here is having a baby." I told her I was really suffering. She asked me to describe the pains and when I did she asked if I had ever taken castor oil before. "Castor Oil! Who gave me Castor Oil? And no I never took it before," I told her.

"I'm the culprit who gave it to you today. I thought you knew what the pre-op med was." Before she finished her sentence, I made a mad dash for the bathroom. Tapping on the door, she asked if I was all right and said she would see me in about an hour. I washed down, changed my gown, and got into bed. This was all too much.

After I was settled, Sister Matilda returned and asked how I was feeling, "Like I just had a baby, Sister." She smiled and said she was not surprised. I said nothing of the voice I had heard. Who would understand anyway? She asked if she could close the door, she had to speak with me about something extremely private. I had a feeling this was about the baby. Did her biological mother have a change of heart? In the past few days that possibility did go through my head. Sister pulled up a chair next to my bed, fixed her eyes on me, and began telling me the most incredible story I had ever heard in my life.

"Linda, I know this is all happening so quickly for you. But sometimes that's how God works. The other night when I spoke with you at the office, you thanked me over and over for considering you and Doctor as adoptive parents for the baby, The truth of the matter is those of us who knew of the situation had no choice. It was out of our hands. God and the Blessed Lady were behind it all. They chose you, not the good Sisters. We were just following their lead."

"Oh Sister, please, you're all so humble to a fault." Sister looked into my eyes and with genuine concern said, "So you can understand the profundity of the situation, Linda, I'm going to start at the beginning. About two months ago, a gentleman came to the hospital wanting to speak to us about his fifteen-year-old daughter, who had just informed him she was seven months pregnant. His wife had died of cancer several years before leaving him to raise three teens alone. Being frightened and not wanting to disappoint her father, the young girl tried to camouflage her pregnancy as long as possible. Needless to say, her father was very sad and visibly hurting for his little girl. Since she was only in her mid-teens, he suggested that the baby be placed for adoption. She agreed. Now, Linda, please listen to what I'm going to say carefully.

"When the father brought his daughter to the hospital to speak to the sisters, he asked that we place the baby with a family we knew could provide the love and security of a happy home. He also requested that the family be Catholic since that was their religious orientation. Both father and daughter absolutely refused to have the child placed with an agency—Catholic or otherwise. It was up to the Sisters to find just the right parents for that baby."

As I listened to Sister Matilda, I honestly didn't hear anything so profound in her story. I definitely was hurting for the young girl who not only lost her mom but who would soon lose her child. In fact, if she changed her mind now, I think I could understand. However, one thing was still puzzling. Why didn't the nuns have a choice in selecting the adoptive parents? Something was missing that I hadn't yet heard. And then it came.

"Linda, after the young girl delivered her baby, the Sisters who knew of the situation knelt around the tiny crib and began praying to the Blessed Family asking for guidance and discernment as to where the child should be placed. In situations such as this, we always pray using the biological mom's full name in our supplication. Praying for direction using your baby's mom's name we heard ourselves saying 'with whom shall we place Linda Marie Bli... baby?' We repeated this over and over until we found ourselves saying 'with whom shall we place Linda Marie Blizzard's baby?' When we realized what we had said a hallowed silence seemed to permeate the room. Instinctively, we knew God had heard and answered our prayers. He had chosen the parents of the newborn who had just arrived from heaven. Can you see why we had no choice, Linda? Your baby's birth mother has your first and middle name and the first three letters of your last name. Who can deny the ways of the Lord?"

While Sister was talking I lay there with my mouth open and eyes fixed upon the face of an angel who had came to deliver a message to me from on high.

When Sister Matilda finished presenting all the details, she asked that one day I tell my daughter about the unusual circumstances surrounding her arrival into our lives. With that she got up, gave me a big hug, and said, "I'll see you tomorrow after your surgery." Watching her as she walked out of the room wiping tears from her eyes, I whispered, "I love you, Sister Matilda, I really do." In the silence of the night I once again sensed the presence of the Lord. Closing my eyes I could feel the power of his light moving through every part of my body as if holding it together. I was suspended in a place I hoped to return to again and again. That night I knew that I would be sleeping in God's arms.

"Mrs. Blizzard, Mrs. Blizzard, wake up! I have to take your vitals and get you ready for surgery."

"Oh my goodness, it's morning already? I can't believe I slept so soundly."

"Mrs. Blizzard, you were sleeping like a baby; I didn't even wake you last night to give you a sleeping pill." Did she say baby? Oh Lord, maybe today's the day I get to hold my baby.

Sister did say the birthing mother would be going home this morning. No sooner had those thoughts gone through my mind when I realized that somewhere on that floor was a frightened young girl who probably didn't sleep at all last night knowing she'd be walking out of the hospital leaving her baby behind.

Would she take one final look as she held her for the last time trying desperately to etch the beauty of her little face into memory? Might she ask to be forgiven for what she was about to do? Suddenly, I realized I had been so wrapped up in my own joy, I never really thought what this young girl might be going through. Never did I wish to embrace anyone as much as her. She needed a mother's warm hug, but none was there. I so wanted to thank her, but how?

Before the tears started pouring from my heart, I told the nurse I wanted to freshen up a bit. In the bathroom I got on my knees, lowered my head, and said, "Father, please allow what I am about to say to be perceived by my baby's birth mom. She needs to know how grateful I am." Whispering softly, I said, *"I'm sending this message to you from the bottom of my heart. Although we've never met, whenever I look into your child's eyes I'll always be aware of the great gift you've given me and the courage it took for you to give her up. I promise with all my heart to teach her as you might and raise her as you would so that one day we can both be proud of the woman she's become. May the pain you feel today be replaced by the joy of knowing that there are three moms loving this special child, you, me, and the Blessed Mother. I pray God's blessing be always upon you, Linda Marie, and may you live in peace knowing you were part of an unbelievable miracle. Thank you for our daughter. Bless you always"*

I had barely finished my prayer when I heard a

knock on the door, "Hi, Lindy, are you OK?" John had come to be with me prior to surgery. "I'll be right out, John, I'm combing my hair." When we had a few moments alone I asked him if the Sisters had told him the story of our baby's birthing mom. He nodded, and said he thought it best Sister Matilda personally tell me the circumstances since she could answer all my questions. "It's a heart-wrenching story, John; one we must tell our daughter when she's old enough to understand."

As I was going up to surgery John looked at me and said, "I have a favor to ask you."

"OK, anything you want, but you better ask now because I'm getting mighty sleepy."

"Lindy, I'd like our daughter to be named Linda Marie after you; there's no better name."

Oh my goodness, I hadn't thought of a name and here my husband wanted our baby named after me. Somewhere between a yawn and a long deep sleep I nodded, thrilled that our baby would share the same name as her birth mom and me. God, how did you manage all this in my unawares?

"Open your eyes, Linda, it's all over, wake up." Sister Matilda's voice seemed so far away. She told me I'd be retuning to my room as soon as the anesthesia wore off a bit. Uh huh, sure Sister, whatever you say," I slurred, slumbering back into wonderland. The next thing I knew I heard my husband trying to wake me to tell me everything went fine, and that

I was back in my room. Opening my eyes I saw my parents and husband, as well as, Sister Matilda and my dear friends from the "white hood gang" standing by my bed.

"Hi, Mom and Dad. Hi, everybody," I said in a rather raspy voice. Sister Matilda, who was standing next to me, looked at me and said, "Linda, I think you missed someone." Feeling still somewhat groggy, I looked and saw her nodding towards my left shoulder. Suddenly I became aware something was there. I tilted my head slightly and there neatly tucked in my arms was my little girl — Linda Marie. Here Sister Matilda had placed her in my arms so she would be the first thing my eyes would see. My God what a moment that was. She was so tiny and still, so beautiful and so mine. At that moment my thoughts went to her birth mother and I prayed thoughtfully, *Please don't worry about your baby, she's safe now. We will treasure and love her as your special gift to us.*

I never saw so many tears in one small room. This time they were tears of unbelievable joy! I had gone into the hospital to be operated on, was given castor oil, had labor pains, went to surgery, and woke up with a baby in my arms. What a lesson I was taught! All along God had heard my prayers, even the most absurd — like wanting to feel a baby in my tummy when I'd had a hysterectomy. He had listened patiently as I rambled on for years wanting to know "what it was like." And to make certain I learned my lesson well, he even went so far as to top it off with three women sharing the same first and middle names. Incredible!

Relating the details of this event is as fresh today as when it happened thirty-nine years ago. Yes, we told our daughter the entire story when she was in her teens. Likewise, the boys were told of theirs. It's always my privilege to tell them again and again the story of their special homecoming and how each child is special to God. Today, Linda has two beautiful boys, Dylan and Drew. Unable to conceive, she and her husband Paul adopted Dylan at three days old. He's now nine and doing great! About three years ago the unexpected happened and Linda became pregnant with Drew. Thank God, the miracle continues in the family. My son Jeffrey and his wife Pam lay claim to their miracle — Zachary, a handsome little boy they adopted from South Korea who is five years old as of this writing. Like a rose is a rose, so a child is a child — a joy to behold. Jay Jay, our first son, remains single and just loves his nephews. In fact, he just loves life. His greatest pleasure is helping anyone in need.

8

A Heady Affair

Brave souls survive a storm:
it's only the spirit
of a body that's worn.

—Linda Luz Benvenue

A household with triplets is, to say the least, hectic but exciting. I loved each day and every second of it. However, when the children were about eight or nine, a medical problem I had since I was nineteen became more severe. Like the endometriosis, it was difficult to diagnose. My husband suggested I see a neurosurgeon. I agreed and made an appointment for the following week.

"Good morning, Linda, and what brings you to my office?"

"I'm not so sure I can describe the problem so easily. All I know is that one minute I can be just fine and the next feel as if a dark cloud is hovering over me and everything becomes dull. It's a strange feeling that effects everything I do for about a week or so. I feel like I'm walking in a fog."

"Can you describe what happens when you feel this way?"

"Well, it's like a sense of uncertainty. For instance, I'll go to the refrigerator to get a bottle of milk, but I'm not sure if what I pick up is actually the milk. It could be orange juice, for all I know. Yet when I go to pour it into a glass it's milk. The same thing happens when I drive, which I try not to do during those times. I see that the light is red, but I'm not sure if it means to stop or go. There's a disconnect somewhere, Doctor. When this fog comes over me I feel as if I'm in a continual state of confusion that dims my senses."

"Linda, I'm going to recommend that we start with some tests, if that's OK with you? I'll give you a slip to have a skull x-ray and some blood work done here at the hospital and see you in two weeks."

"Good enough! I'll see you then, Doctor"

Within two weeks, I went back to hear the results of my tests. "Your blood work was all within normal limits, Linda. However, your skull x-rays shows an abnormality on the right side of your temple directly above your ear. It appears to be some type of growth. As I explained to your husband this morning, we need to do more specific testing to determine its nature." After hearing the word "growth" I blocked everything out of my mind except the words "pneumoencephalogram" and "psychological testing." He was suggesting I have both done. Leaving his office, I ran up to John's hoping he wasn't seeing patients. When he saw how distraught I was, he felt helpless to do anything to comfort me. He knew well what a pneumoencephalogram entailed and what I was about to go through, and so did I.

As an x-ray technician I was quite familiar with the procedure, having assisted with several of them. It involves removing all the fluid from the spinal column and injecting air via a syringe up through the column into the ventricles of the brain. X-rays are then taken of the air filled ventricles to visualize and identify any suspected anomaly. The procedure is horrific! Since the patient's cooperation is needed for the x-rays, no anesthesia is administered. Now it was my turn to be on the other end of the syringe, not as the physician's assistant but as the patient.

Although I was given a mild sedation in pill form, I was well aware of what was happening. When the fluid was drained from my spine and the air injected, my head felt like an overfilled balloon ready to pop. I knew I was going to pass out and told them. When I came to I had this awful pain in my head and couldn't stop heaving. They proceeded to take x-rays of my skull from every angle possible as I sat harnessed to a chair that kept me upright.

The pain I felt in my head was beyond excruciating. I understood what people meant when they'd say, "I just want to die." Both the severe head pain and the heaving lasted more than two weeks. This procedure is no longer allowed to be performed, thanks be to God. About three weeks later and after completing a battery of psychological tests, it was time to revisit my doctor and hopefully find the cause of my unexplained episodes. For support, I asked my mom to come along.

As suspected, the doctor informed me there was something suspicious on the right side of my brain that appeared to be a type of tumor. His recommendation was brain surgery. Although he was sympathetic, he was also very concerned with the findings of the psychological testing. The report indicated that I was a borderline mental defective with a present IQ that was in the low eighties, with that number probably decreasing within the next five years. It was my doctor's opinion that my decreased IQ was the result of the tumor.

"What's my prognosis, Doctor, if I have the surgery?" He looked at me squarely in the eyes and said, "Honestly, Linda, I can't tell you that because I simply don't know. Brain surgery is risky and it's difficult to accurately predict the outcome." Leaving his office, I said I'd get back to him. I had a lot to think about, and needed to talk to my husband, who wasn't at the hospital at that time. How grateful I was to have my mom with me as we drove home both frightened for what the future may hold for me.

When John arrived home that evening he knew by the look on my face that I was definitely down and mightily scared. I told him I really didn't want to talk about it right then, but maybe later. My poor parents kept calling to make sure I was OK. I told them not to worry that I'd be just fine. Did I really believe that — absolutely not! But in a few days my tune would change

Thank God our kids were at school when the following occurred. It was about one in the afternoon and since Gin was off that day, I decided to do a little straightening up starting with the living room. The suit jacket my husband wore the previous day was draped over a chair. I removed it to hang in the closet when a rather large envelope fell out of the inside pocket. Picking it off the floor, I noticed it was addressed to my husband from the neurosurgeon and had the words "private and confidential" typed in the lower left-hand corner. At first I stood frozen trying to decide what to do. But then I did what any normal housewife would do — I opened it! What I read was basically some of what my doctor had told me, but hearing it and then reading it are entirely different, believe me.

My psychological report was completely detailed. As I read through the pages I was saying to myself, "Who are they talking about? This is certainly not me, no way!" I kept shaking my head repeating over and over "No! No! No!" until I let out a "No!" that was so thunderous it seemed to come from the bowels of the earth. It was a shocking denial of the facts! With fists clenched, I shouted out, "This is a cruel thing you do, God! If the situation were reversed I'd never think of doing this to you. In one breath, you satisfy my every desire; in the next you take them all away. How can you do this? And what about the children you gave me to raise? How can I do that if brain surgery leaves me crippled, blind, or both?" But none of that seems to matter since my IQ will be so low in a few years I'll be dumb and really won't know the difference or even care. God, all I ever wanted to do was to be a mom and finish the job." With no more to say I lay down on the sofa and cried until the well of tears went dry. I feel asleep feeling emotionally spent.

Not sure how long I slept, I got off the sofa to check the kitchen clock when I became aware something had drastically changed and it was me! Where did all the anger and hostility go? Why didn't I feel depressed or sad? After all, I still had the same medical problem and IQ. What happened while I was sleeping that I was ready now to face life with a new resolve? I went around the house somewhat in a daze until the children came home from school. I was never happier to see them, and I loved it even more when they called me, "Mom." After John arrived, I told him of my decision. "No surgery for me! I don't care what any of the tests show, I won't change my mind, either."

I told him I had read the report and of the emotional explosion that followed. I tried to explain that what was upsetting me was knowing I had to make a life-threatening decision with absolutely no certainty of its outcome. I felt as though there were two doors staring at me in the face and I had to choose one of them — door number one, surgery, or, door number two, no surgery. I wanted him to know that after I awoke, I had this "sense of knowing" that everything would be OK. Somehow while asleep, God engraved upon my heart the most profound meaning of his providence. *"Linda, don't you know it's not the door that's important, it's trusting and believing in my boundless love for you. No matter which door you might have opened I would have been there. I'm behind any door you choose in life. I'm always there, always faithful in my loving care of you."* When I began to question why I felt differently, I knew I had the answer necessary to make the decision I did. The words I heard were not audible — it was as though they were written on a teletype in my brain and I simply repeated word for word what I saw. It wasn't strange or weird at all; it had happened to me before. I'm convinced when we sleep, God takes the opportunity to talk to us uninterruptedly about issues that lay heavy upon our hearts. Many nights before I drift off, I'll say, "Speak Lord, I'm listening."

Anyway, with all the above under my belt, I was confident I'd always be under God's watchful eye. Even though I still had episodes of confusion, I knew he had everything under control. About a year later John came home and told me of a neurologist that had just joined the staff at the hospital. He had excellent credentials and John suggested I see him.

What a wonderful, caring man. After a review of my medical history and a thorough neurological examination, it was his opinion that I should be admitted to the hospital for a battery of tests. He would reserve his diagnosis of my problem until all reports had been reviewed. Two weeks later I was admitted for testing.

I had no idea what could comprise a battery of tests. Talk about thorough! There were oodles of blood tests measuring this and that, skull x-rays, and those dreaded psychological tests that in themselves took more than two days to complete. With everything finished, my doctor informed me that nothing showed up as being abnormal except for the psychological testing; however, the results were the same as those done several years prior. My IQ, though low, had not changed. Yippee! Interestingly no changes were evident in my skull x-rays. The abnormality seen in my right temple area was still evident and appeared to be the same size. I was happy my doctor was pleased with most of the findings but I couldn't share in his feelings and told him so. "Doctor, I have to be honest with you. I believe my husband is beginning to think at this point it's all in my head. He's insinuated some things that really hurt. I know how I feel! When I'm in a foggy state it's impossible for me to comprehend anything I read. Nothing makes sense." After blurting that out, he said, "Linda, I'd like to make a small correction here. Whatever is wrong is definitely in your head, and I'm determined to find out what it is. One thing I'm certain of, it's not your imagination. I've ordered one more test before you go home tomorrow. You've had it done many years ago, but I think it's time to have it repeated. Let's keep our fingers crossed something shows up." "What test is that, Doctor?" "It's an electroencephalogram. It's not painful, as you know, and can be very revealing." I told him I wasn't worried at all.

That night unable to sleep, I knew it was time to do some soul searching. "Father, I'm concerned they won't get to the bottom of my problem, and I don't want to look stupid in John's eyes. You and I know something is wrong. Lord, I trust implicitly in your loving providence. If a cause is not found I accept it as the road I am to travel. Whatever the outcome of tomorrow's test is, it's all right with me." With that said I went peacefully asleep.

The next morning after my final test, John stopped by and said I'd be going home in a few hours. I was happy I'd get to see my children, but disappointed that I might not have a concrete diagnosis. Just about then my doctor came in and asked if he could speak with my husband. They walked out into the corridor and after ten minutes only my doctor returned. "Where is John?" I asked.

"He told me to tell you he'd be back to take you home as soon as I write your discharge summary, Linda"

As soon as I heard him say "discharge" my heart sank. I guess that's it, I thought to myself—the scan was negative. My doctor sat on my bed, grabbed my hand in his and said, "Linda, you have epilepsy."

"Epilepsy! But I don't convulse, Doctor."

"Your scan showed abnormal spiking of your brain waves. It appears with the symptoms you exhibit you have a non-convulsive type of seizure disorder called petit mal."

"Does that mean I don't have a brain tumor? What about the psychological reports that indicate I'm a borderline mental defective?"

"One thing at a time," he said. "Right now let's start with what we know. I'm going to prescribe a medication that may help reduce the severity and frequency of the episodes. It's called Dilantin. Let's see how you tolerate it before we proceed with anything further."

"Thank you so much, Doctor. John will be very relieved and happy to hear this"

"That's why I wanted to see your husband alone. I reviewed the findings with him and asked that he try to understand what you've been through the past years. Linda, he appeared deeply concerned but relieved that finally there was a definitive clinical diagnosis."

Finally, I thought to myself, at the age of thirty-five I have a name to put to the condition. It had been a long stretch of uncertainty — sixteen years to be exact. Although I continued to have seizures they were less intense and infrequent, for which I was grateful. Eventually by the time I was in my late forties they completely subsided.

With all the kids in middle school and with me not working for John in the evenings since he now had a secretary, I decided I wanted to teach religion to Catholic children attending public school. After taking the prescribed classes recommended by the archdiocese of Philadelphia, I became a certified CCD (Confraternity of Christian Doctrine) teacher and was on my way. How wonderful it was being able to teach children ways to relate to God at such a young age. I loved it and knew God had me right where I was to be. Little did I know these gatherings were to be the springboard for what was to happen next.

Interested in learning, I continued taking classes

at a religious center nearby focusing mainly on topics dealing with the Judeo-Christian writings of the Old and New Testament. I would devour books dealing with Christology and theology. I couldn't get enough! Then one Sunday morning a really bizarre thing happened. My mom called to say she'd love to have the kids for the day. After Mass I dropped them off and drove home. Being alone with no distractions was wonderful! After finishing up a few projects, I had a very strong urge to read my Bible, which often meant I was about to learn something I needed to know. As usual before opening it I said a short prayer. "Father, I feel you drawing me to read and listen to your Word. Help me understand the message as it relates to me." With no thought I opened to Genesis, Chapter 28, and read verses 1 through 22. What I read left me dumbfounded. Although I knew I was directed to read that section I didn't know how to absorb its meaning.

The story is about a dream the Patriarch Jacob had while sleeping in a place called Bethel. Resting his head on a stone, he dreamt he saw a staircase reaching up to heaven and back with angels going up and down. Standing next to him was the Lord saying he would bless him and all his descendants. "I will be with you and bless you wherever you go, and will bring you back to this land. I will not leave you until I have done what I promised you." When Jacob awoke the next morning, he thought the place to be the House of God and the staircase being the gate that opens into the heavens. He took the stone he laid his head upon, poured olive oil on it, and set it up as a monument dedicating it to God. Here is the sentence that literally made my head spin. "In dedicating the monument, Jacob named the place Bethel, which was once known as Luz." If I read that passage once I read it ten times thinking I was mistaken. How could this be? How was it possible that my name was in the Bible, especially an uncommon name like "Luz." My maiden name was Linda Luz. As I lay prostrate on the floor I felt bewildered. I knew I was led to read that passage for a reason. But what did it all mean and what are the odds of finding your name in Scripture? Years later I would come to find the answer to that.

One thing I must say, God certainly knows how to set the stage when there are lessons to be learned and prophecies to be foretold. Example: My mom and dad seldom took all three children for the day—they were a handful, but she said she wanted to give me a break. And John, who usually comes home from the hospital about noon on Sundays, arrived at three-thirty saying he had two emergency admissions. Coincidence? Perhaps, but I think if I had a glimpse into God's planner I'd see all the above listed as "things to do."

9

Now or Never

Unfolding ourselves layer after layer
makes us feel like a stage with no player.

—Linda Luz Benvenue

During the next several years, the idea of going to college and getting a degree went through my head. I wanted to learn so I could teach others the ways of God. It was John's sister, a Notre Dame de Namur Nun, who would often say, "Linda, you have such a desire to teach, I think you should go to college and get a degree in religious studies." Oh Sister Jane, I would think to myself, if you only knew how much I want that as well.

You have to understand, Sister Jane was one of those brainy people who taught mathematics to high school students. She had no clue about my IQ deficiency and I wasn't about to tell her. Although I'd listen as she detailed the advantages of a degree, I never let her know I wouldn't be able to make it academically. For sure, it was pride that kept me from admitting the truth. I was flattered, however, that she thought I was college material.

But, Sister Jane being a dedicated nun never gave up. "Linda, what have you got to lose? Remember, God works through people, so why not give him a chance to work through you? Believe me, you won't be happy until you try." That did it! That one hit home. The next morning when talking to God, I asked if Sister Jane was right. "Is that your direction for me, Father — college? Let's not forget, I'm not nineteen, I'm thirty-nine. Plus, there's the issue about a little thing called IQ. Remember that?"

Whenever I need some spiritual light thrown on a particular situation, I usually peruse the scriptures. That was my intent after speaking with Sister Jane. As I bent over expecting to pick up my Bible that weighed about two pounds, I found myself holding instead a Missalette, which is a small book containing all the readings and responses for most Masses and weighing only a few ounces. Emblazoned in bold letters on the cover, no more than five inches from my face, were the words "The stone rejected by the builders became the corner stone." I sat there staring at those words until my eyes became blurry. As usual God had heard and answered. It was his way of telling me not to rely on what the world or others believe to be truth, but to look within myself where the spirit of truth resides waiting to reveal itself.

The next time I saw Sister Jane I told her she was right and that I wouldn't be happy until I gave college a try. I promised I would search out schools in the area that week. I did and found one I thought would be perfect — Our Lady of Angels College in Aston, Pennsylvania. It was run by the Franciscan Sisters and located only fifteen minutes from home. Since it was already August, I knew I had to hustle and get some information since school would be starting soon. I called and asked for a brochure and an application, which I received in several days. Looking over the material I was very impressed and could see myself there as a student. I was now ready to discuss my new venture with my husband.

John was receptive but a little concerned that at thirty-nine the rigors of college might be a bit much for me. Plus, the children had to be considered. I told him I'd take classes only when they were in school, but if I did happen to be a little late, Gin, who was working for us full-time, would always be there. He said the final decision was mine but questioned how I would handle the academics with my IQ problem.

Remembering the quote from scripture regarding the cornerstone, I told him I had to see how much I was capable of learning. If I had major difficulty then I would walk away graciously from the academic world knowing I had at least tried.

We both agreed that I had to be absolutely honest and up front with the admissions office regarding my medical issues. The following morning I called my neurologist asking if he would send me a letter explaining my medical problem so I could present it to the person who would interview me. Within a week, after filling out the application, I received a call from the school. "Hello, is this Linda Blizzard?" "Yes, it is." On the other end I heard someone say she was from the admissions office and wanted to set up an appointment for an interview. I got so excited I was tongue-tied. Within four days I found myself driving to the place I hoped would one day be my alma mater. My fingers were crossed.

Walking into the college I became a little leery and wondered if I could pull this off. I wasn't used to talking about my medical concerns with anyone. Now here I was going to blab to a total stranger. I started thinking maybe I was pushing the limits of my ability a little too much. Why should I complicate my life? It's a great life! Did I really need this degree anyway? Having a bewildered look on my face, I heard someone say "Can I help you, Miss?" I turned and this rather tall nun with a broad smile was looking directly at me. I said "hello" and told her I was looking for the admissions office. "Would that be for registration?" she asked. I nodded and smiled. "How wonderful! If you follow me I'll take you there." Oh dear Lord, I thought to myself, she's treating me as if I'm going to be accepted. What a good feeling and great moment that was. But now here I was sitting down ready to be interviewed by another nun.

"Good morning, you must be Linda Blizzard." "Yes, Sister, that's me." "OK, let's get started," she said. She had my application on her desk and proceeded to ask me a few questions. She had received my high school transcript and told me everything was in order. Interestingly, she never once mentioned the fact that I was an "older" applicant. Placing my papers aside, she asked what my aspirations were and why I had chosen their particular college to pursue my goals. I told her of my interest in religion and spoke about other things she might want to know. However, pressing at the back of my head was the thought "Get it over with, Linda, tell her about your fears and stop wasting time. Show her the letter from the doctor explaining your medical problem. She has to listen."

Taking the letter from my purse I handed it to the nun. "Before you read it, Sister, I want you to know that I'm prepared for whatever your decision may be regarding my admission as a student here." After reading the letter, she looked at me and said, "This must be very hard for you to do." With a lump in my throat, I nodded and knew I was free to talk to this stranger about my fears.

When she heard what I had to say, she asked me to please be seated in the waiting room, she wanted to confer with the Dean. Good grief, not the Dean! I began thinking how easy it would be to avoid this whole situation by simply walking out the door I came in. Within ten minutes, Sister returned and invited me to accompany her to the Dean's office. My goodness, this might be worse than I thought. With no explanation I found myself seated in front of the Dean. "Well, Linda, Sister explained your situation and after reading the letter from your doctor I agree there is a bit of a problem here. When I heard the word "problem" I thought, "Here it comes." I wanted to tell her then and there, "Sister, you won't be hurting my feelings if you think I'm not qualified to be a student here. Actually, it would be a relief."

She proceeded to share with me her philosophy. "Linda, I happen to believe that problems are meant to be solved. What may seem like an obstacle may be a solution waiting to be uncovered." Many of our female students have situations that need special consideration. I think we might have a solution that may help yours." What she told me took my breath away.

"We certainly want you as a student at Our Lady of Angels College (later changed to Neumann College).However, at this time, I think it best that you be enrolled as a non-matriculated student." Asking her to explain, she told me initially I wouldn't be enrolled as a candidate for a degree. I could take courses but wouldn't be subjected to the testing. Basically, she was saying I wouldn't get any credits for the courses I took. Her recommendation was to proceed cautiously by taking one course each semester for a year to see how I fared. If after that time I was confident I could succeed, then I would be enrolled as a matriculated student working towards a degree. "What do you think about that, Linda?" "Sister, I think that's just great! Does that mean I can start this September?" "Absolutely! No need to wait any longer," she said, smiling.

As I was leaving she assured me our conversation would be kept confidential as well as the fact that I would be registering as a non-matriculated student. I was also informed that she would periodically review my records. Leaving her office, she looked at me and said, "Linda, if you ever have a problem please see me, I know together we can work it out." Problems? What problems? I thought to myself. I was finally a college student — matriculated or not didn't matter. I was there to learn and the Sisters of Saint Francis would teach me.

Before going home, I found my way to the chapel; there was a lot to discuss with my best advisor and I laid it all out. "Father, the Dean wants me to take one course at a time both this semester and the next.

At that pace I'll be graduating with my kids, if I'm lucky. I'd like to take a few more courses. What the heck, if I'm going to fail, I'll fail big." With my eyes fixed on my hands that were folded on my lap I became absolutely startled when I heard these words ringing in my ears. "I WILL GIVE YOU WHAT THE WORLD CANNOT. BELIEVE THIS!" They were so loud they caused me to shake my head several times in disbelief. This time I wasn't frightened by the familiar voice. As always the message was direct and clear. Responding, I said, "Father, how can I not believe? You gave me two beautiful sons, and a daughter whose birth I felt I labored through. The world did not do that, you did. And what about John? If I hadn't heard the words "this cannot be," I would have married someone else. Your words have been directing my life for a long time. You have already given me what the world could not and I am grateful. But are you telling me now there is still more to come? If there is I gladly accept and welcome it. Bring it on!"

As I sat in the pew, I began thinking about my dilemma regarding the course or courses I should take. It seemed now that if the world said one, God was saying some. With a feeling of confidence, I slowly got up from the pew and started walking down the aisle when my eyes fell upon the most beautiful marble statue of Our Lady. From my earliest days I've had great devotion to her. She is the nurturer, the listener, the gentle advisor who loves us all. I knew I would return to that chapel many times if just to sit, be comforted, and listen.

I couldn't wait to get home and tell everyone the good news. My children were thrilled and saying things like "Hey, Mom, now we can help you with your homework and even pack you a lunch." We all laughed. It seemed everyone was happy for me. I'll never forget what my dad told me. "You can do it, dear, just believe." There was that word again — believe. How I loved the sound of it.

When it came time to register for classes, I was anxious to meet some of my classmates. I only hoped someone my age would be part of the freshman class. Arriving at school there were signs directing us where to go. It was all so exciting! Looking around, it appeared that I just might be the oldest student there. But it didn't seem to matter, everyone was so friendly. Phew! What a relief. Looking back now they were probably feeling sorry for me. Hah! Talk about misinterpreting the moment.

I was in a bit of a quandary when it came time to select my courses. Which do I choose? I didn't want to override the Dean's suggestion; however, believing in God's plan to "give me what the world could not," I decided to take three courses — a Religion course for the Dean, an English course for me, and a Philosophy course for "you know who." I sure was anxious to put "believe" through its most arduous task. Well, with books in hand and a badge identifying me as a student clipped onto my jacket, I waved good-bye to my new friends and said I'd see them on the first day of class.

How quickly the first few months flew by. I was busy with my head in the books. Did I have problems understanding some things? Absolutely. I'd go over and over the material until I thought I knew it well enough to take the exam. That's right, I chose to participate in all assignments and testing. After all, I wanted some idea of what I was or wasn't capable of. As far as matriculation, no one — not even the instructors — knew I wasn't matriculated. I guess my pride didn't want them to find out either. All I'd say to myself before any exam was "Believe, Linda, believe."

What a great feeling it was having the first semester under my belt. What a wonderful relief! By the middle of January I received my grades. Talk about being beside yourself. Religion — A; English — B; Philosophy — A. I must have checked that envelope ten times to make sure I was the intended addressee and there was no mistake. Nope, that's me all right! God, you sure did give me what the world could not.

One of the first things I did was call my neurosurgeon and tell him the good news. Although he was happy, he felt it was time for another round of psychological testing. Perhaps the findings might have changed. Well, they didn't. My doctor called and said, "Whatever you're doing just keep it up; we'll take another look in a year or so." I decided then and there — no more testing! As I saw it the world was waiting for me to fail while God on the other hand was saying "not on my watch."

I still can remember one of the more memorable moments of my first year. When I returned for my second semester, I noticed lots of students gathered around the bulletin board. Wondering what the heck was going on as I made my way up front, I heard someone say, "Good job, Linda." I said "thanks" but had no idea why. Another said, "Nice job, Blizz." When I got close enough to read what was on the board, my head began to spin. I was totally shocked. There it was as plain as day — Linda Blizzard, Dean's List. I had made the Dean's list! I had no idea such a list was posted for your classmates to see. I have to say I felt humbled and proud. Humbled because I knew I hadn't done it alone and proud because I had listened to "someone" who asked that I hang in and "believe."

Before long I was going into my second semester of my sophomore year and had to select a major. I knew I wanted religion studies but at that time no such major existed. I chose to major in the humanities concentrating on religion. By this time I was taking four courses a semester and loving it. Somewhere during the first week of that semester, I was paged and asked to go to the Dean's office. I'm sure you can imagine what was going through my mind.

Thinking I was in trouble for taking more than one course over the last three semesters, I wondered how I was going to explain myself. Very carefully, I thought, very carefully. When I arrived at her door, she was extremely cordial and gracious as she invited me to have a seat. She started asking me questions that had nothing to do with my matriculation. "Linda, I've been looking over your records and I think you could carry a second major. What do you think?" Was I losing my mind? Wasn't this the same nun who wanted me to take one course a semester for a year and is now asking me to consider taking on a double? "Do you think you can do it, Linda?" Still with no mention of the matriculation issue I said, "Well, Sister, if I can't, I know someone who can help," as I pointed to a picture of the Sacred Heart that hung on the wall behind her desk. She smiled and understood completely. As to what other major I might select, I told her behavioral science would be my choice. She asked me to explain. I told her that I believed that knowledge of human behavior works hand in hand with the tenets of most religions, and that the ministry of Jesus exemplified that beautifully. His success was helping people discover new patterns of behavior that would move them from being passively to actively involved in creating a new vision for themselves. He raised their hopes by raising their expectations — one value, one behavior at a time. I reminded the nun what Jesus told the lame man he healed at the Pool of Bethzatha. "Listen, you are well now: so stop sinning or something worse may happen to you." Sister nodded her head knowing where I was coming from and where I wanted to go.

Senior year, I couldn't believe it! I had made many friends at school including many of the Sisters. So many good things happened that I was overwhelmed and always humbled. I won the first elocution contest held at the college. My talk was entitled: Women as Priests. Reading the judges comments one wrote "I thought I was listening to a professional speaker. I was captivated." I was asked to organize the first prayer group at the institution, which I did. And believe it or not was asked by the Dean to participate in a twelve-member think tank sponsored by a major corporation. I loved it all! Looking back, what I loved most was the awareness that God and I did it together a step at a time. It was vital for me to always let him know that the only moment that was important was the one at hand. After all, when you get your cues from such an authority, it's best to behold each moment as Divine.

A while before graduation I was called to the business office. The nun in charge asked me this question: "Linda, you're graduating with two degrees and both are in the Arts. You don't need two diplomas, do you? Isn't one sufficient?" I looked at her and without any hesitation said, "No, Sister, believe me, one isn't. I need two — one for me and one for God. We both earned it."

Graduation day was absolutely beautiful. My whole family was there. I was so happy. But the happiest moment came when my name was announced over the loud speaker. Walking up to the podium, I heard, Linda Marie Blizzard, BA, BA, Magna Cum Laude. With two degrees and graduating Magna Cum Laude, I graduated near the very top of my class. Walking back to my seat and raising my two diplomas to the sky, I said, Thank you, Father, you kept your word and gave me what the world could not. As I move forward now help me to teach others to believe as you've shown me.

As far as my matriculation, I never did ask the Dean. I just figured somewhere along the way I became matriculated and was never told. Today on my college transcript the only reference to that issue is that I'm listed as a "special student." I'll toast to that! Regarding my IQ? As far as I'm concerned, IQ no longer means intelligent quotient but illusive quirk. From that point on I never thought about it again.

For the purpose of chronology, I started college in 1975 and graduated in December 1980. The graduation exercise itself was not held until June 1981.

10

The Fatima Happening

The illusory will often entrap;
not so with truth,
'tis neither packaged nor wrapped.

—Linda Luz Benvenue

With college under my belt in December of 1980, I had six months before my official graduation exercise to be held in June of 1981. Since I was free my dad's family discussed the idea of taking a trip to Portugal. It was his deepest desire to sink his feet into the ground he once walked as a young child. Sharing his Portuguese descent, I thought the idea sounded great! In putting the itinerary together we all agreed there was one place that was a must to visit — Fatima, the place where Our Lady appeared to the three peasant children in 1917. Since we would be in Portugal during the middle of May, it was planned to visit Fatima on the thirteenth, the anniversary of the original apparition. We made Lisbon our home base, which we were told was about two hours south of Fatima. With all plans in order our small group of seven including my parents, three aunts, a friend of my parents, and myself left in May 1981 for what would become one of the most remarkable experiences of my life. Landing in Lisbon was indescribable. Walking off the plane we all gathered around my dad to get a sense of his feelings. Putting my arms around him, I whispered, "You're home, daddy." Choked with emotion, he didn't say a word as he walked with his head lowered, thinking I'm sure of his parents who had passed on many years before.

Arriving at our hotel we spoke with the concierge and asked if a meeting could be arranged with the person who'd be driving us to Fatima. Within a few hours we found ourselves huddled around him as he told us he'd gladly take us to the shrine, but in his opinion visiting Fatima on the feast of the apparition was not advisable. His explanation was that on the anniversary date the roads are so congested with cars and people trekking up the mountainside that driving to the entrance would almost be impossible, and we'd have to walk the last mile or so up the mountainous road. We sat there shocked! That was not what we wanted to hear. He might have taken the wind out of our sails for a brief time but Aunt Mary spoke up and said, "If we have to trek, then that's what we'll do. But we are going to Fatima on the appointed day and that's that!" We all chimed in "Amen."

On the morning of the thirteenth I got out of bed excited and anxious for the day to begin. As I walked toward the window to let some light into the room, I saw drops of rain trickling down the panes. Can't be, I thought, it's probably stopping. With the drops becoming more and more persistent and the sky grayer, I thought, "C'mon, Lord, You can do better than this." Going down for breakfast I knew the one person who'd be delighted to see the rain — our driver.

Sure enough, when we had gathered in the hotel lobby, he informed us that he wasn't about to drive us to Fatima in the pouring rain. Besides, the roads would be treacherous and could only complicate matters. It wasn't his idea to jeopardize our safety or our health. We all looked at each other hoping once again someone would speak up. As far as I was concerned, it really didn't matter. I could wait another day or two; after all, the Lady wasn't going anywhere. My main concern was for my mom and what effect the rain might have on her arthritis. If she had a flair up she could end up in bed for days. I certainly didn't want that to happen. Well, who do you think was the first to speak up? Yep, my mom. She told the driver she wasn't going to let the weather spoil our plans and was confident the rain would stop. She told us not to worry, she'd be just fine. Returning her gaze to the driver, she politely asked if he would be kind enough to have someone else from his company take us to the Grotto at Fatima. Way to go, Mom, you tell him! Looking somewhat perplexed, he turned to this tiny woman barely five feet tall and ninety pounds, and said, "Little lady, if you have it in you to make this trip on such a day as this then who am I not to drive you and get you back safely." He shook his head saying, "I must be crazy to do this and I'm not even a Christian! With umbrella in hand, our now happy group got into his van and off we went to see "the Lady."

Talk about anticipation. All your life you hear stories about the Blessed Mother appearing to children. Now here you are at the foothills of that sacred place and your head is filled with questions. Why were these children chosen from all the rest? Why did it happen in Portugal and not America? What were the secrets they were not to reveal? Does innocence always play a part? Finally, the ultimate question — could I ever see her? Of course the age-old answer to that as we were taught in school is "we are not worthy."

Be that as it may, I was happy to be visiting Fatima and paying homage to someone I considered a real part of my family and a dear friend. When my children were babies and all crying in the middle of the night, I'd often ask her to please quiet one while I tended to the others. It worked! We always seem to have a great working relationship even to this day.

Riding in the car, I looked around at our small group and wondered what personal reasons we each might have for wanting to be in Fatima. Certainly my mom was hoping that through Our Lady's intercession she might get some relief from the pain her arthritis caused. Aunt Annie would offer prayers for her two daughters, Celeste and Lisa, as well as praying for her own peace of mind and well-being. Her husband Sal died many years before leaving her to raise the girls alone. Aunt Esther's only son, Louis, would receive all the pray power she could send as would her husband Lou who suffered from chronic neck pain. Aunt Mary's focus would be praying for her deceased husband Leo and her sister Dora, who not wanting to leave her husband Leonard, who disliked flying, stayed home. As for my mom's friend, Marie, who came along on the trip, I'm not sure who the recipient of her prayers might have been. One thing I was certain of — my dad would offer many prayers of thanksgiving. To be with some members of his family in Portugal was more than he thought possible. He was a very simple man and a humble one at that. As for me, family headed the list. There were also friends who asked that I intercede on their behalf. I had a list tucked neatly in my purse ready to retrieve when at the Grotto.

Driving in the rain was mesmerizing. Most of us were lost in our own thoughts. I was wondering what this day would hold for each of us. What impressions would we come away with that might have a lasting effect on our lives? Before that day ended each of us would be affected by the happenings. About a quarter mile from the Grotto, we noticed some people walking on both sides of the road. Our driver seemed a bit surprised but very pleased by the fact it had stopped raining and he could drive us directly to the Grotto. Where were the crowds? It looked a bit empty to me. Being deposited at the entrance, we told him we'd be back in about five hours or so. "Take your time; I'm here whenever you want to return to Lisbon."

When you visit a holy place you don't know quite what to expect. One thing you can be sure of is seeing lots and lots of people. Not so today — at least not yet. As we continued walking through the entrance we saw people ahead of us. It wasn't until we turned left and walked directly into the Grotto or Shrine area and there they were — masses and masses of people. I would not be exaggerating if I said there were more than a quarter of a million people directly ahead of us all praying the rosary. I stood there in total amazement not moving a muscle. Where had all these people come from and why didn't we see evidence of such a multitude as we were driving? I looked for my mom to make sure she was all right and then asked that we all stay close together.

Standing where we were, the crowd made it difficult to see what was happening towards the front. As I slowly scanned the crowd, I was spellbound by the overall reverence of the people. It touched my soul watching them pray the rosary with their beads devoutly draped between their thumbs, their heads tilted toward the sky. The men had on drab black suits that were somewhat worn and tattered with shirts that had lost their whiteness years ago. The women were dressed in long black dresses and most had some type of head covering. To see this sea of black was moving.

We were later told by our driver that most of the pilgrims were peasants who had traveled many, many miles just to be there at that special time. From where stood I saw very few Americans. There was one group, however, you just couldn't miss — ours. Both my Aunt Mary and I had on bright plaid blazers that would blind you if we stood in the sun. Someone else in our small entourage wore a loud green jacket with big flowers embroidered on the front and back. Looking around I was beginning to feel more than slightly self-conscious and was glad we were standing behind everyone.

Perusing the area where the original apparition took place was impossible since I wasn't sure where to look. I did notice beautiful white buildings surrounding the Shrine that gave the whole area a very pristine feel. Way up front stood a long white altar that seemed to sparkle as the sun peeked through the clouds. And to the right of it was the statue of Our Lady raised high on a platform.

Honestly, up to that point, I found it difficult to say one single prayer — the pilgrims held all my attention. Many of the Portuguese — men and women alike — had skin leathered by the sun and hands that were large, thick and gnarled from years of laboring in the fields or at sea. Although it was hard to directly see their faces, I could sense that in their hearts they were speaking to the beautiful lady. As thoughts crowded my head I heard a man directing the people to move ten feet to their right so aisles could be created for the sickly and crippled to be carried down to the altar, which was about four hundred feet from where we stood. Within minutes I saw children in wheelchairs and on stretchers brought down the dirt path to where the statue of Our Lady stood. The elderly — many with crutches and in wheelchairs as well — were slowly processing down. Nurses in white uniforms were accompanying the severely ill to the front. Oxygen tanks were being rolled along the sides of the sickly and many had tubes protruding from their bodies.

The most heart-wrenching moment came when I caught sight of women crawling down the path on their knees with their sickly children in their arms. Dressed from head to toe in black dusty clothes these women were oblivious to the crowds as they inched their way trying to get to the altar and near the statue of Our Lady. Looking at their faces, I couldn't help being drawn to the deep folds that seemed frozen in determination and courage. Their eyes glistened with a resolve reflecting their optimism. Nothing could stop them from placing their petitions before the Blessed Mother. With the hope of a miracle awaiting their little ones they would go on a few feet more. Mesmerized by their strength and with eyes gripped on them, I let out a rather deep and loud sigh of disbelief. With tears running down my face I was to utter the last words I would say that day at the Grotto at Fatima. Before telling you what I said you have to understand what I was feeling.

Looking at the pilgrims I became keenly aware of their spiritual valor and humility and sensed they had something I didn't. They seemed to possess a spiritual richness far greater that I could ever imagine. Among them I felt spiritually impoverished, spiritually poor. I kept wondering if I would have gone down on my knees and crawled along some dirt path all that distance to pray to the Lady? Or would I have relied on my Western logic convincing me that the heavens wouldn't want me to make a fool of myself? After all, if God is omniscient and omnipotent, then he can hear my prayers and supplications no matter where the location or the position of my body.

With feelings of utter isolation running through

me, I realized the tears dripping down my checks were not for the peasants but for me. I felt lost and insignificant amongst them. Lowering my eyes these were the last words I whispered to God that day, *"Lord, You don't even know I'm here."* How was it possible to feel so sad at such a holy place? The entire service lasted about two hours, during which I didn't say a single prayer or offer any petitions to Our Lady — not even those requested by my friends back home. It was the faces of the worshipers imbedded onto my mind that continued to hold me captive.

When Mass was over and the crowd began to disperse, we wandered about for a while then decided it was time for lunch and some good Portuguese food. We had been advised by our driver that the Fatima Hotel, a short walking distance from the Grotto, was a great place to eat. What a charming place! When I sat down I was amazed at my hunger. Not only did I eat what I had originally ordered but finished what remained on my mom's plate. It didn't take long for me to sense that my hunger was more than physical.

As we sat around the table we talked about our experiences at the Grotto. When asked what I had felt, I simply said, "I don't know," and admitted rather sheepishly that the last words I had spoken were, "Lord, you don't even know I'm here." My dad looked at me rather puzzled until I said, "Daddy, what happened out there touched my soul deeply. I was shaken because I learned more of the truth of me." Actually what I really wanted to tell him was that I felt so left out and detached from God at the service we had just attended. Plus, I'm not so sure I could ever do what those women did. Does that make my loving God conditional? Not saying a word, my dad nodded and smiled. I think he understood.

Following our lunch a stroll was in order, so we decided to go searching for souvenirs to bring family and friends back home. As I was walking through the little streets I kept thinking to myself, "Here I am perusing the Fatima shops looking for something to recount an experience I never felt part of." We must have shopped for about two hours before deciding it was time to head back to our car and waiting driver.

Everyone was excited about their purchases, so naturally back in the car it was show and tell. We each had a turn showing others our purchases and revealing the name of the lucky recipients. The gifts ran the gamut from rosaries to holy water, books to medals, and of course small statues of Our Lady. When it was my turn I opened a lunch-size white paper bag that held within it eight smaller bags — each no more than two inches square. Merchants, being very frugal, hand out bags that fit the size of the purchase. I passed each little bag around for everyone to look at its contents There was one bag I couldn't wait to have them open. It contained two 18K gold medals I bought for my husband and me. After all the bags were passed back, I realized I was missing the one with the gold medals. I looked through each little bag several times making sure the gold medals hadn't accidentally been misplaced within another bag. Finally, I spoke up and told everyone my dilemma. "My gold medals are missing and aren't in any of the bags. I definitely saw the clerk put them in a bag before placing them in the larger one with the others, but they're gone! I can't believe this!" With that my mom said, "Linda, let me check your bag, maybe you just missed it."

When she finished her rummaging, she admitted the bag containing the medals was missing. Everyone except my dad had a turn checking for the missing medals. Zilch! The driver, sensing my concern, said he wouldn't mind driving back to Fatima and to the shop where they were purchased. His thinking was that perhaps they had somehow slipped out of the bag and someone at the store was still holding them. Since we were only about twenty minutes from the Shrine everyone thought it wise to return. I agreed.

Driving back to Fatima and feeling a bit down, I had little to say. Nothing was working the way I thought it would. As far as I was concerned I might as well have stayed home. Holding the large white bag on my lap, I began thinking once again how distant God and Our Lady seemed at that moment. I can never forget the awful sense of loss I felt in my stomach. It was such a sick feeling. Turning my gaze to the mountains I had a strong urge to look inside the big bag one more time. Putting my hand near the opening, I immediately felt something in my palm. Turning my hand over, I opened it and there resting in my palm was a small, white perfectly smooth bag — unlike the others that were all crinkled from over-handling by almost everyone in our group.

Absolute disbelief grabbed at me as I slipped its contents into my hand. There resting securely in my palm were my two missing gold medals. Stunned, I let out a gasp and was lost in a dimension more real than my own. From a spiritual chasm within myself I heard a familiar voice saying clearly and slowly and with loving concern, *"I KNOW YOU ARE HERE, LINDA."* Clasping my fingers around the medals I tried to chisel into memory the moment the unseen became seen and the lost found. As I continued staring at my precious medals, I instinctively knew that in one split second I had witnessed LOVE reveal itself in its natural and supernatural state. My medals hadn't been lost at all but were suspended in a dimension not visible to me. It was LOVE that made them reappear. Uncompromised and uncondensed without complication or condition, LOVE was capable of making the unbelievable believable by the creative energy derived from the purity of its intent. In that instant I knew God took whatever action was necessary to show me the multidimensional aspects of his infinite love for me.

Sitting there holding my two medals, I felt I was

clutching the hands of God, who had heard me say not long before that I doubted his awareness of my presence at the Grotto. How sad is the heart that is capable of speaking words of ingratitude to a loving Father. At the Shrine, against a backdrop of humble peasants, I was flooded with feelings of unworthiness and began sliding into a sea of doubt and fear. Were the humble peasants more worthy to be loved by God than me? Being deceived by what I thought was more pleasing behavior to the Lord, I became spiritually oblivious to what he wanted to show me and so I became mute to prayer. By materializing his love for me God wanted me to know unequivocally he did not see me as I saw myself. I had made a hasty judgment based upon deception. I was looking at my human frailties and its many imperfections while God saw only my Divine Perfection. After all, isn't it true that we're made in his image and likeness and that where God abides so abides perfection?

At the Grotto I believed what my eyes beheld to be true. As a result, I couldn't sense the Divine within me and therefore was unable to utter a single salutation. It's funny, I had gone to Fatima hoping like most to be touched in some way by the experience; little did I know that initially I was the obstacle preventing that from happening. I guess we all build walls to hide behind.

What I received from that miraculous event has had a tremendous impact on my life. When questions arise about the existence of God, I simply look down at my palm, close my eyes, and recall his words to me and say, "There is no doubt." While others scramble for an explanation, I rest secured. Oh how to pass that feeling on to the world. Please, God.

There were other valuable and important lessons birthed at Fatima. First, another person's physical posture while praying or paying homage to the Divine in no way invalidates my own. Whatever position I choose to take when in dialogue with the Lord in no way diminishes the intent of my prayer. Whether or not I would crawl on my knees down some dirt path is of my own choosing and has nothing to do with God. Rather, it's the intent of a love-filled heart longing to express its deepest affection to the Divine that will always be pleasing and spark a response from the God within.

Second. My God is never hidden from me. Of course I wish his appearance was more human than ethereal. I identify with the Divine through spiritual fusion and not physical association. It's through the merging of spirits that I can proclaim the Father and I are one. Through the "now you see them, now you don't" medals, God was trying to say, "When you think I'm not there never doubt, never fear, only know I am."

Third. For years I guarded the gold medals, keeping them in a safe place never wanting to lose them because of the significance they held. One day, the unthinkable happened. They disappeared again — gone! Where? I had no idea. After months of lost-and-found praying I had the gnawing feeling that the Lord wanted to enlighten me on the medals. Opening my heart I was made aware of a truth that never would have come to mind. Since Fatima my focus had always been on the miracle of the medals. However, I was shown that what happened that afternoon had nothing at all to do with the medals — they could have been bottle caps for that matter. God would have used whatever was at hand to get my attention to bring my heart in unison with his spirit so we could joyously commune once again. The miracle was watching Divine Love penetrate the observable world in such a way it couldn't be denied. I was witness to God using whatever he could to bring a smile to my face and leave inscribed upon my heart the depth and sincerity of his love for me and everyone.

Lastly, and most importantly of all, in life there are times when doubt finds its way into our daily routine, and we become frightened of the possibility that there may be no tomorrow; that death may very well be the end of the line and any imaginings of life beyond this one are futile. Not so my friends! Not so! When doubt grabs at you, then you grab onto God. Speak to him of your fears. Visualize him next to you and listen to what he wants to tell you. I can almost predict you will hear the same words I did at Fatima,

"I know you are here." Isn't it interesting—and I think of it often—that those words do not focus on a time or place but rather on pure consciousness and its awareness of presence of being? "I know you are here" suggests we are in the same place as God. The "here" insures that the past, present, and future are all part of a "now" reality submerged within the eternal presence of God.

How long I sat in the car in a dazed state as we headed back to Fatima, I can't be sure. It wasn't until Aunt Esther, who was sitting next to me tried to get my attention by nudging me with her elbow, did I finally bounce back into the present moment. She knew something had happened since I appeared shaken and teary eyed; I slowly opened my hand showing her the two gold medals. "My God, where did they come from?" she exclaimed. With that everyone looked back to see what was going on and listened intently as I related, as best I could, what had just happened. Needless to say, everyone wanted to touch the medals. Our driver was beside himself and commented, "I've been taking people to Fatima for over twenty-five years and never have I witnessed such an incident as this. I may be a Jew but even a Jew knows a miracle when he sees one. OK, my little pilgrims it's time to head back to Lisbon and feast."

After dinner and a brief walk around the city, I was tired and ready for a good night's sleep. I'd had a day that was now part of my forever. All I wanted was to be alone with my thoughts, my God, and my medals. I fell asleep holding onto them for fear they might disappear. When I awoke the next morning little did I know what would be in store for me on such a lovely day.

After breakfast we all gathered in the lobby to discuss the day's agenda. It was a free day and we could choose to do whatever we wanted. Several in the group chose to peruse the shops and outdoor markets of Lisbon; others just wanted to rest after the previous day's journey. Aunt Mary had something else in mind. She wanted to return to Fatima a second time and asked if I'd like to join her. Without hesitation, I said, "Yes! Oh yes, please let's go. I have some unfinished business to attend to."

Since we were the only two who would be going and since our driver was off for the day, we asked the concierge if it was possible to find someone to take us back. Looking at me, he said, "I heard what happened yesterday at Fatima; I'm not surprised you want to return. And yes, I do have someone to take you there if he's available." After a quick phone call, he returned smiling and told us to wait in the lobby; within the hour we'd be on our way back to the Grotto.

I must say the second time around was almost as unbelievable as the first. We had a charming Portuguese driver who listened with great interest as Aunt Mary told him of yesterday's events. Having heard of a myriad of mystical phenomena this was a first for him. As we were approaching the Grotto, he asked if we would also like to visit places very few get a chance to see. Aunt Mary and I started asking questions. We couldn't believe our ears! We looked at each other knowing we were in for some day.

Our first stop was the Grotto. I couldn't get over the fact that twenty-four hours previous it had been packed with people. Today told a different story. With only four or five hundred pilgrims roaming about we were free to roam the area imagining how it might have appeared in 1917. It didn't take long for me to utter prayers of joy and delight knowing God was my constant companion. Before leaving the Grotto I read the petitions my friends from the States had given me and then said my own final prayer at Fatima. "Lord, thank you for showing me that as your perfect creation I am perfectly loved. I know now I needn't look upwards or outwards for the presence of your company, I need only go within."

When we returned to our car our driver said he wanted to take us to a special place not far from the Grotto. Within a short time we found ourselves at the little village where the visionaries were born. We sat mesmerized as our driver filled us in on the local history of the town and its people. Getting out of the car, my eyes glimpsed an open doorway with an elderly woman dressed in black sitting there on a straight wooden chair praying her rosary. As we walked slowly by her, she never glanced our way — so intent was she on the vision she held in her heart. Asking who she was, we were told she was distantly related to one of the visionary children.

As we meandered through the little town our driver graciously introduced us to some of the townspeople. We felt extremely privileged to be photographed with several and to be invited to visit the home where one of the visionaries had lived. It was a very humble abode indeed with its low ceilings, stark walls — save for a few religious pictures hanging here and there — and meager furniture. Walking through the rooms was surreal. You could almost imagine the chatter of children trying to explain to their parents the image of the beautiful Lady they had seen on the mountainside.

Walking along the cobbled stone roads towards our car, I stopped to gaze once more at the old woman sitting in the doorway. She hadn't moved and her composure hadn't changed. She sat still and silent. I thought perhaps she had fallen asleep praying but that mattered little. I sensed she'd slipped into a dimension where to her delight she found herself nestled in the arms of the angels. Staring at her I knew she would become an immutable memory I would need in order to regain my spiritual sanity as I flitted about my world doing busy stuff that probably didn't matter anyway.

Driving back to Lisbon my heart was filled with admiration for a simple people who shared so much.

Isn't it always the way that those with so little can give so much? Through them I experienced first-hand what being alive is about. Their genuine modesty bespeaks their belief that "it's when you're giving that you're living." Such sentiments rose not from the depths of their pockets but sprang from their heartfelt desire to express LOVE as it sought to express itself through them. When conveyed simply, sincerely, and with a grateful heart such love is beyond price and is instantly felt by its recipient.

The happenings that occurred at Fatima made me aware that as God had reached out making me conscious of his Presence, I wanted to help others become cognizant of the same. The question was where and how do I start?

11

A New Vision

A mind with little vision
is locked in its own little prison.
—*Linda Luz Benvenue*

After returning from Portugal in May of 1981, I decided I needed time to absorb what I had learned, not just from the events at Fatima but from my life thus far. What came out of the next several months were lots of questions and one certainty — God loved me just as I was and went to great extremes to prove it. Were other people of that conviction? Could they feel his love even if they didn't profess loyalty to any religion? Or did others believe that God loved those best that strictly followed the dictates of their professed faith? For instance, my heart still breaks when I go to Mass and observe the pain of those unable to receive the Eucharist (Communion) because they have divorced and remarried. They'd sit in the rear of the church, heads down, wishing they'd disappear as the Eucharist was being distributed. I saw many get up from their seats and walk out of the service feeling humiliated by the exclusion. Oh God, help me to understand, please. Is full participation in the Mass, including receiving the Host, only for those Catholics who comply with the rules, and is reception of the Eucharist the reward for compliance?

In the midst of doubt I'd recall the passage in scripture regarding the incident between Jesus and the woman at the well. That particular lady had been married many, many times yet Jesus offered her his "cup of life" saying basically that she'd never thirst for love again. Interestingly, she wasn't even a Jew but a despised Samaritan. Doesn't a law of exclusion tend to make people feel humiliated and less worthy to be loved by God? Another question arises then — was the Jesus of Palestine who lived over two thousand years ago more sensitive and compassionate than the Jesus of the Roman tradition, the Jesus of modern times?

Many of the above issues and questions continued to swirl around in my head and as a result were the springboard for the formation of New Visions, a

Christian Growth and Scripture Study Community I began with the help of several friends in August of 1981. The pastor of the parish, Monsignor Stevensen, was very supportive and pleased that a Bible study program would be available for those wanting to learn more. It's no big secret that the majority of Catholics do not read the Scriptures.

With the formation of New Visions, my goal was to emphasize the simplicity of God's love as I understood it and as it was expressed by Jesus in the New Testament. I wanted the people to know the Lord doesn't care if we're not all rocket scientists with IQs above one hundred and thirty. His focus isn't on our humanness with its deficiencies but on the disposition of our heart and its desire to reflect his love to others. I feel strongly that God offered me a love that was totally uncomplicated, one I could understand, one that wasn't dependent on my ability to pass or fail a test. How I hated to hear the words "God's testing you." As far as I'm concerned he doesn't test anyone; if anything, what He does is try to strengthen us, any way he can.

From the onset of New Visions I knew that the depth and breadth of my work would be endeavoring to make the incomprehensible, understandable to anyone needing assurance of the Lord's love. Moreover, I wanted people to meet — maybe for the first time — the God of their inner dwelling who was there waiting to embrace them at every moment. I felt strongly that New Visions could be the perfect venue for the coming together of God and his people.

What an exciting time! The pastor continued to offer his full support and saw no problems with our ministry. Initially, we met once a week with scripture being taught and issues of concern by those in attendance discussed. Within a few months, visiting the sick and dying in private homes and hospitals became an integral part of the ministry. Eventually, New Visions held its first half-day retreat at the parish in Wallingford, Pennsylvania, and shortly thereafter extended its meeting to include another on Sunday evenings. A lot of time went into the preparation of the lectures and weekly teachings. I was grateful I had that time to devote to it.

While I prepared all the teachings, my friends took care of other activities that certainly helped New Visions run smoothly. We were all volunteers choosing to work gratis for the Lord. Any donation we received went into an account and was used for snacks, paper goods, and the like.

Within seven months I was giving retreats throughout our area and had the honor of being invited back to my alma mater to give retreats and inspirational talks to students and nuns. What a joy it was for me to return to where it all began. It was during this time that the people attending New Visions wanted to broaden their understanding of the history of the Holy Land and questioned the possibility of visiting Israel. I told them New Visions was up to its ying-yang in activities, and it would be best for them to find a travel agency or contact the archdiocese of Philadelphia for information. As far as I was concerned — and I was adamant — New Visions was not getting involved in providing pilgrimages to the Holy Land, and that was that!

"Ladies and gentlemen, welcome aboard El Al Airlines' nonstop flight to Israel landing at Ben Gurion Airport in Tel Aviv." On June 13, 1982, a group of twenty-five people from New Visions, including myself, were off to dig our feet into the earth God had chosen to cushion the steps of his Son. Yep! Our ministry now included retreat pilgrimages to the Holy Land. I will never forget that first trip.

Before the arrival of our plane, I was sitting in the El Al terminal at JFK Airport in New York observing the Israeli security walking up, down, and around with their submachine guns under arm. It suddenly dawned on me that we were headed to a country that was at war with Lebanon, and I was the one responsible for the well-being and safety of the group. Holy cow! Whenever my eyes caught sight of the soldiers' guns, I become traumatized, thinking, "These men are not tin soldiers, they really mean business. I'd feel a little better if they'd only smile once in a while. Oh God, what are we doing here? I must've totally misinterpreted your vision for our little community. Definitely, I've gone too far this time. Forgive me, Lord, for my eagerness."

With such thoughts running in my head, I glanced up to see an Israeli soldier looking directly at me and headed my way. My heart beat so fast I couldn't catch my breath. Being approached by a man and his gun isn't the norm. The soldier stood directly in front of me and asked if I was Linda Blizzard. I so desperately wanted to say, "Who?" I nodded and he asked if I would please follow him. Did he honestly expect me to say "no"?

Everyone nearby was looking in our direction, and I felt I was being eyed as a spy or seen as a member of some covert operation. He led me to a station where I was literally interrogated. "Are you the leader of the group New Visions traveling to Israel?" Admitting my guilt, I was asked to explain the reason for the trip and to state to the best of my knowledge the occupation of all those traveling with me, especially the men. Good Lord, do they think someone in our group is a spy? With my voice in a whisper, I told them that we were all innocent travelers going to the Holy Land to visit Jesus. As soon as I said that, I knew it sounded corny but I was as nervous as a mouse on a cat farm. The inquisitor and the soldier, still with guns, looked at each other and smiled assuring me that what they were doing was all part of security and perfectly normal. If they thought that made me feel better they were wrong. As soon as I was free to go I ran straight to the ladies room.

If you're asking how they knew I was the leader

of the pack, they found a brochure with my name on it in a member's bag. Asked where I was seated, she had pointed me out. Snitch! End of story, at least at the airport.

Our journey to the Holy Land was remarkable. In the fourteen days we were there we traversed the small country covering both the land of the Old and New Testament — from Galilee north to Judah in the South. I had a priest, Father Frank, from the States, join us as our spiritual advisor. He was wonderful and was himself awed by the feeling of just "being there." The Masses he celebrated each day were a blessing for the group. I could go on and on about some of the happenings of that first trip; that's right, I said first. Two more excursions were to follow annually each spring until it was no longer safe to travel to the region.

When it was time for our second pilgrimage, I asked my son Jeffrey, who was sixteen at the time, if he would like to join me on the trip. He was thrilled but questioned, "Why me, Mom, and not Jay Jay or Little Linda?" Good question and a caring one at that. My response to him was simple and one he accepted and appreciated.

When Jeff was five years old, it was discovered he had Legg-Perthes disease of his right hip. Basically, the ball of his thighbone wasn't getting enough blood supply and that caused the bone to die. Needless to say this condition was painful especially when he walked. He was admitted to the hospital and placed in a full body cast, which was the treatment back then. Being only five and unable to move was absolutely frightening for him. With more hospital stays, casts and steel braces holding his leg in place, it would be almost four years before he could walk on his own without the aid of some type of support. During those four years, Jeffrey spent at least two lying on top of a mattress in his cast on the living room floor. Since I wanted him close by me all the time that seemed the best place to watch over him. At night I'd sleep next to him on the sofa barely an arm's length away.

When Jeff was about ten and fully recovered from his problem, I came down with what I imagine was the flu. I was so sick one evening I couldn't make it to bed and so fell asleep on the sofa. About three in the morning, I awoke realizing someone had placed a pillow under my head and covered me with a blanket. Lifting myself off the sofa, I felt something at my feet. Looking down, I couldn't believe my eyes! There was my Jeffrey all curled up on the hard floor with nothing covering his little body except the pajamas he wore. I reached to cover him and as I did he woke up. I asked what he was doing on the floor and he said, "Mom, when I was sick you slept beside me on the sofa. Now that you're sick it's my turn to watch over you." With warm tears filling my eyes, I asked if he was the one who put the pillow under my head and covered me. He smiled and my little Nordic prince looked at me and said, "Go back to sleep, mom, you'll be OK in the morning." For all the aforementioned, I wanted Jeffrey to join me and be part of the Holy Land experience. And what an incredible experience it was for both of us.

Having my son with me made my second venture to Israel more personal. Our passenger list was comprised of twenty-four eager individuals including a totally blind young woman whose stamina was as remarkable as her spiritual disposition. Before I proceed, I want to say that many of the questions I had held in mind for a long time were answered. However, little did I know that in that distant land they would come in such an explosive manner?

The spiritual advisor for our journey was Father Joe, with whom Jeffrey roomed. A second priest, Father Rene, wanting to be part of our pilgrimage, joined us. We felt doubly blessed having two servants of God with us. Since this was my second trip, I was more familiar with the land and some of the customs of its people. There were a few familiar faces I remembered and who remembered me, like shop owners and innkeepers. It's so very warming to be remembered when you're so far from home.

With the success of the previous year's journey, I chose to have the same Israeli guide accompany us throughout our trip. Daily he and I would meet for a half-hour after dinner to review the next day's agenda. It was then we'd discuss appropriate places for me to give a teaching.

The first part of the trip was spent in the Galilee area, where we stayed at a kibbutz guest house in Tiberius — Nof Ginossar, set on the water's edge. After a full day of touring we'd return to our charming dwelling to enjoy a delicious meal prepared with most foodstuffs organically grown at the kibbutz. About an hour after dinner we'd gather around the lake for reflection, song, and prayer. That hour held an indescribable peace even for a sixteen-year-old. Everyone wanted to relate their impression of the land Jesus loved. With the hour spent and people gone it was my time to sit there with my son contemplating the night and its images.

A very touching experience for couples traveling with us was having their marriage vows renewed at Cana. At the request of his mother, Jesus performed his first miracle there while attending a wedding. With our accompanying priest presiding at the Mass each couple vowed once again their loyalty to each other. The bride wore a white mantilla that I had brought from the States and carried a bouquet made of lovely ferns and flowers indigenous to the area. The couples looked radiant as they repeated their "I do's" with a deep sense of love and commitment. Nary an eye was dry as we sang and hailed them, asking the Lord to bless them all their days. Following the ceremony we celebrated with wine, and this time it didn't run out.

After three days in Galilee it was time to head south towards Jerusalem, where we stayed at a lovely guest house just inside the Jaffa Gate and within the walls of the Old City. This was to be our home for the remainder of our sojourn in Israel. The Old City reeked of times past with ancient artifacts visible everywhere. Days were spent retracing the steps of Jesus both inside and beyond the city. It was during this time that I personally became witness to some astonishing events — as I saw them to be and still do.

Our Israeli guide was very sensitive to the needs of our group. One evening while discussing the plans for the next day, I happened to mention to him that my maiden name was in the Bible. He looked at me somewhat confused but listened intently as I proceeded to tell him what had happened to me on a Sunday afternoon many years ago as I lay praying and reading the Old Testament. He immediately picked up the Bible and started reading the passage from Genesis 28. Looking at me, he asked, "Is that why you're here in Israel because the Lord spoke to you about this land?" Shaking my head vigorously, I told him, "Absolutely not! I never wanted to travel here the first time, let alone the second. Somehow these trips took on a power of their own and here I am." The poor guide kept nodding, but I felt certain he really didn't understand my confusion regarding the whole experience. Or did he?

Several days later, in the morning, he asked if he

could discuss something with me. I nodded and listened as he told me something I never expected to hear. "Linda, your surname Luz in Hebrew means almond tree. The rod or staff that Moses carried when leading his people was probably made of that wood. Do you think God was trying to tell you years ago through the passage you read that one day you would be leading people here to the Promised Land?" I looked at him flabbergasted and thought to myself, "Is it possible that even before I went to college God was directing my path that far into the future?" Our guide took out his Bible and read the passage. For those unfamiliar with the text, I've included it below. The particulars are important for what was to follow.

"Jacob left Beersheba and set out for Haran. When he had reached a certain place he passed the night there, since the sun had set. Taking one of the stones to be found at that place, he made it his pillow and laid down where he was. He had a dream: a ladder was there, standing on the ground with its top reaching to heaven: and there were angels of God going up it and coming down. And Yahweh was there, standing over him, saying, 'I am Yahweh, the God of Abraham, your father, and the God of Isaac. I will give to you and to your descendants the land on which you are lying. Your descendants will be like the specks of dust on the ground; you shall spread to the east and the west, to the north and the south, and all the tribes of the earth shall bless themselves by you and your descendants. Be sure that I am with you; I will keep you safe wherever you go, and bring you back to this land, for I will not desert you before I have done all I have promised you.'"

Jacob awoke from his sleep and said, 'Truly, Yahweh is in this place and I never knew it!' He was afraid and said, 'How awe-inspiring this place is! This is nothing less than a house of God; this is the gate of heaven!' Rising early in the morning, Jacob took the stone he had used for his pillow, and set it up as a monument, pouring oil over the top of it. He named the place Bethel, but before that the town was called Luz.

Jacob made this vow, 'If God goes with me and keeps me safe on this journey I am making, if he gives me bread to eat and clothes to wear, and I return home safely to my father, then Yahweh shall be my God. This stone I have set up as a monument shall be a house of God, and I will surely pay you a tenth part of all you give me.'

After our guide read the passage, he looked at me in earnest and said, "This is a journey you need to take, Linda. You've come this far, and I think it's time you go to Bethel. First, I need your permission and full understanding of the situation before I set it up." I couldn't imagine what he was talking about and asked him to be more specific. He told me that several weeks prior there had been some unrest in the area of Bethel. However, he felt certain it had subsided and our journey there would be uneventful.

I told him I'd definitely have to speak to our group, explaining my reason for wanting to go, and I'd leave the decision to them. In any event, our guide had me convinced that while I was in Israel I should make the attempt to find out what was mine alone to discover, even if it meant going with only my son and him. When I met with the group to explain the situation everyone felt it was important that I go, but not alone. They all wanted to accompany me. I was humbled by their dedication but also concerned for their well-being and my son's. The following afternoon we headed to Bethel, which was about fourteen miles north of Jerusalem, fortified with the prayers and blessings of our two wonderful priests on board.

We were certainly a very happy group, singing most of the way and looking out at the terrain. About fifteen minutes into the trip our bus came to an abrupt stop throwing all of us forward in our seats and strewing whatever was overhead throughout the bus. Some people sitting on the end seats were pushed to the floor. Immediately, the bus was bombarded with large boulders that seemed to come from everywhere. Our Israeli guide yelled for us to take cover on the floor, then directed our driver to open the bus door. In an instant our guide jumped out of the bus and pulling a gun from his pocket began firing shots in the direction of the hurling rocks. The sound of the gunfire was deafening and frightening. Looking around to make sure no one was injured, I noticed that several of the bus windows had been completely shattered. I was really terrified that we would be the victims of an angry mob who definitely wanted to harm us. The shots continued to ring out for about five minutes. As I turned to make sure there were no major injuries, the words God had spoken to Jacob began to resound in my ears at such a volume they overshadowed the reality of what was happening at that moment. *"Remember I will be with you and protect you wherever you go."* I stared out the window absolutely spellbound and totally shocked that the God I couldn't see knew I was in trouble and wanted me to know he was going to keep his end of the promise. He had spoken to me with loving concern as he had done many times before. With the intensity of his words fading, I rejoined the present with a confidence that defied explanation. I knew we would all be fine. Thankfully, no major injuries were sustained, only minor scrapes and bruises.

I later discovered the reason for the abrupt stop our bus had made. The perpetrators had placed large spikes in the road hoping to flatten the bus tires bringing it to a halt. If that had happened, we would've been sitting ducks and open victims of their revenge. Our bus driver, being acutely aware of the area and of a similar incident that occurred weeks prior, spotted the spikes and instantly jammed on the brakes, which sent us all flying.

With the incident over, our driver immediately

radioed Israeli army headquarters informing them of the situation. Within ten minutes they arrived with guns and tanks ready to resolve the incident. We all watched as they used their submachine guns to shell four houses they were told the boulders were projected from. Windows and doors were punctured with rounds and rounds of bullets. This went on for almost twenty minutes. The army had delivered their message loud and clear. I was aware of no casualties; those responsible had fled.

One of the soldiers in charge asked if several of our men would volunteer to accompany them to army headquarters and fill out an incident report. Of course my son Jeffrey just had to go. "Please, Mom, I saw the whole thing." Being almost sixteen, he wanted to see what headquarters looked like. I gave my consent knowing that four men from our group who had volunteered would take good care of him. Besides, the echo of God's words was still with me. We would all be fine.

When everyone returned from headquarters our guide was very apologetic and said that on behalf of the Israeli government and in lieu of what had happened to the American Christian travelers, a thirty-day curfew was to be placed on the town, meaning no one was allowed in or out of the area after seven pm. Thanking him for what he had done, I asked why he had been carrying a gun. He smiled saying, "Most Israelis carry guns wherever they go; it's a way of life here. We live with two sets of eyes — one in the front and the other in the back. We are always on guard."

After we were all settled our guide said, "OK, let's get started again. It's off to Bethel."

"Bethel? No way," I shouted. "Oh yes!" shouted my group right back. "We want to continue on with the saga of Bethel." So we proceeded to our destination and was I ever so happy we did. As I said before, you don't go ninety miles in a hundred-mile race and quit — at least not in this land. So off we went to pay a visit to the "House of God," which is the meaning of Bethel.

Approaching Bethel our guide suggested we park the bus at the bottom of a knoll and walk to the top. There were some trees in the area under which we stopped and I gave a teaching regarding the contents of Genesis 28. I told everyone they were free to wander about but to please be back on the bus in thirty minutes. Since it was very hot most sat under trees drinking water and enjoying the leisure time, especially after what we had just been through. As for me I was definitely caught up in Jacob's dream until I heard Father Rene call down to me from atop the hill.

With glaring sun, I looked up and thought I saw two young boys standing there with the priest. Walking up to them I wondered what two boys who looked no more than thirteen would be doing there since no houses were visible for quite a distance. "Shalom, and how are you?" I asked, as I reached the top. Both boys nodded, smiled, and said "Shalom." Father Rene looked at me for what seemed like a very long moment, then said, "Linda, I've been talking to these two young men since we got here and learned something very interesting I think you need to hear." "OK, Father, and what is that?" He pointed to the boy on his left and asked that he tell me where he was from. Immediately I thought what a stupid question to ask this boy. He certainly looked like all the other handsome Jewish young men we saw. His hair was short, curly, and dark. His eyes, big and round, were framed by the longest lashes any little Miss would die for. His olive complexion completed the picture of an intelligent, warm, Middle Eastern teen. He smiled and said he was Israeli and was preparing for his Bar Mitzvah to be held soon at the Temple in Jerusalem. I was so happy for him and related the same. Did I say he also had the most beautiful smile I ever saw with teeth so white and bright?

With the sun almost directly in my eyes it was difficult to clearly see the boy standing a bit behind and to the right of the priest. I asked Father to have him move closer to where the other child was. When he did I looked up to see a fair-skinned, rather slim young man with a mop of curly red hair atop his head. "Oh my, don't tell me, let me guess. You're from Ireland!" He shook his head, I tried again. "OK, you're from America!" Again he shook his head. Finally I said, "Well, just where do you come from and where did you get that gorgeous head of hair?" Then came the moment when I new why I was meant to be in Bethel, Israel. "I am not an Israeli; I am from Brazil here to attend my cousin's Bar Mitzvah. I am a Portuguese Jew."

I was absolutely dumbfounded, and unable to speak; my eyes were rolling in tears. Father spoke up and told the boy that I too was Portuguese. Looking at me and thinking I spoke the language, he said something I didn't understand but had the feeling he thought it a bit strange to meet another Portuguese at Bethel. Father pointed to me, and said, "Her name is Linda Luz." With that the boy nodded his head saying, "Yes! Beautiful light — your name means beautiful light. It's true!" In silence I took his hands, held them in mine and whispered "thank you." I'm sure he had no idea why I appeared to him to be sad when actually I wasn't. I was in awe and couldn't believe what had just transpired between three total strangers. As I turned to leave they both said, "Shalom." I clenched my right hand, placed it over my heart, bowed my head, and walked down the hill looking for a place to be alone.

When I came to some stones I picked them up, then went down on my knees and remained solemnly silent. It wasn't a time for words; I had been guided to that place years before and I simply wanted to bask in the presence of the Lord as did Jacob. I felt divinity all around me. Before leaving, I lifted my head saying, "Father, like Jacob I will go wherever you send me trusting always in your concern for me. I have built an altar with these few stones but I've no oil to anoint it. Please accept my tears as a symbol of my commitment to you. I seal it with the love pouring out from my heart."

Immediately that moment became my personal "covenant" moment when God and I bonded "in spirit" at a level I still find hard to describe. There was a certainty that nothing I could ever do would change that. What a relief the awareness of that was. It was a covenant bonded in love and sealed in trust and wasn't based on human accomplishment. With all my peculiarities, imperfections, and many weaknesses I was loved as "me" and knew nothing I did or didn't do could ever excommunicate me from God. From the church — Yes! From God, never!

12

Moments of Truth

Man's hope is best sustained
by seeking the truth
from those who have gained.

—Linda Luz Benvenue

The experience at Bethel was a pivotal point in my life for a number of reasons. First of all, I had a clearer vision of my place within the Source of Life. With that assurance I was no longer afraid to question the absurdity of things that have absolutely nothing at all to do with my love for God and vice versa. Secondly, I was free now to accept truth as it was given to me by an Infinite Being that had communicated with me, making my relationship with him dynamic and not static. Lastly, I was awakened to the fact that my movement towards the Divine was ultimately a call into self-discovery. I knew the voice of the caller to be that of God's leading me to experience my own divinity. This is not without some struggle at times.

After years of indoctrination into certain beliefs and practices held by family, friends, and church, it's often hard to change mindsets. When I was young I believed what I was told and that carried over into my adulthood. For instance, as long as I can remember the words "I am not worthy" were spoken by everyone professing to be Catholic. You not only said it, you believed it as you lowered your eyes and head feeling a sense of unworthiness. I also believed there was a big bad angel out there called Satan who was out to get me and if I wasn't careful he would. Growing up with the personal experiences I had of God, I become aware that he had a different idea of who I was and wanted me to know it. In time I came to realize that much of what I had learned earlier was gleaned out of fear. No longer afraid, I knew the only safeguard against setbacks was making certain I didn't affix my sights on the fallacies of an outer world bent on confounding my vision and holding me captive if even for a minute. Little did I know my awakening would intensify in the Old City of Jerusalem as we walked under the "Arch of the Ecce Homo" (Behold the Man) and onto the Via Dolorosa.

Whenever I traveled to Israel, I always arranged to have a Mass celebrated at the Chapel of St. Mary Magdalene located near the place where Jesus fell the first time. The sanctity of that little chapel was penetrating.

Before Mass everyone in the group sat quietly, caught up in their own thoughts about what had happened almost two thousands years before. During Mass, especially at the Celebration of the Eucharist, it was obvious that each brought to the altar their deepest act of love. It was during this particular rite that something hit my heart with an overwhelming thud.

Prior to receiving the Host, the priest says, "This is the Lamb of God who takes away the sins of he world. Happy are those who are called to His supper." Catholics everywhere respond with the words I previously mentioned, "Lord, I am not worthy to receive you. Only say the word and I will be healed." I was shaken to my soul and unable to say one word, let alone respond. It was as if I became a mute. My God! I can't say those words anymore! You, Father, have shown me that I am not only worthy but deeply loved. Am I now to deny that? As I knelt there I remembered all those experiences I had gone through with the Lord, especially at Fatima. All I could do now was trust in him and not the words I was told by others to utter. It was a major awakening for me.

There are only two questions to ask. Did Jesus die

because we are unworthy? Or because as children of the Father, we are truly worthy of everything he freely wants to give us, especially his endless love, forgiveness and compassion. Certainly, if anyone could understand the weariness and disappointments of life leaving him to feel rejected, and unloved, might it not have been Jesus? After all, wasn't he counted as one of the kids on the block of scanty means? Didn't they scoff at him? Nonetheless, he never fell into the trap of feeling victimized by his circumstances. He never felt unworthy! Why? Because he knew he was loved unreservedly by the Father. It was this that allowed him to accomplish what he did. By focusing his energy on the capacity of the human heart to love and forgive, he was able to scattered seeds of hope into the most dreadful of conditions. By raising the inner awareness of those he met, he awakened people to the possibility that change was possible.

Look at the Apostles; he even made them feel worthy! Love makes all worthy, even the birds of the air. To suggest we are unworthy cancels out the good one man did during his lifetime. Jesus loved everyone into wholeness — all the way to the cross. His life reeked of love not judgment. HE LIVED, LOVED, AND DIED BECAUSE WE ARE ALL WORTHY! He came to earth to deliver that message. We are winners from the start! Why? Because God's love is a worthy love and it is from such a love we were formed.

You may ask if I received the Eucharist that morning in the Chapel of St. Mary Magdalene. I did. But I did not utter the words "I am not worthy." Then, as now, before receiving the Host I simply say, "May my worthiness be seen in the light of the Son who lives in me and the Father who continues to create through me," and end it with, "thank you for teaching me your way of loving that promotes peace without prejudice." With these words and sentiments I receive my Lord humbly and in truth.

Perhaps one day the words said during Communion will be changed. All I know is the truth of me does not lie in the outward appearance of my fleshiness with its foibles, frailties and fears, but lives within my soul where rests the glorious mystery of my Godlikeness.

During the entire time we were in the chapel something very peculiar occurred. I couldn't shed a single tear even when contemplating the passion of Jesus. I thought perhaps I was blocking out the horrors of that tragedy. Sitting there focusing on the "why's" of my feelings, I suddenly sensed an awareness creeping into my consciousness — one I hadn't previously considered: "DON'T REMEMBER MY PAIN, LINDA, REMEMBER THE GAIN." It was like a huge signpost flashing in my head that had nothing to do with feelings of unworthiness but with feelings of guilt and remorse.

Being taught early on that "He died for my sins,"

made me feel bad and I remember wishing there was a way I could take Jesus down from the cross. Whenever I focused on Calvary, I was moved to genuine sadness and believed it was my sinful nature that kept him there. Like most obedient Catholics when I was young I'd take my place in the confessional line at church every Saturday afternoon, offer my litany of sins to the priest, ask for forgiveness, then hope the admission of my transgressions was sufficient enough to abate at least some of his suffering. I remember on numerous occasions when I was eight or so and unable to remember what I did wrong. I'd fall back on the previous week's list of grievances, already confessed and forgiven, hoping God wouldn't notice. Can you imagine? It wasn't until my experience at that chapel in Israel that I knew for certain that Jesus wouldn't want our point of focus to be on the pain and anguish of the cross, not when he spent his life trying to alleviate the pain and suffering of others. Sitting in that chapel I knew that focusing on His pain would keep me on my knees, while looking at the gain would have me always on my feet ready to serve. Another awareness awakening my spirit to the truth was emerging. As regards my desire to take Jesus down from the cross it remained with me for a very long time and took many years before I was ready to tackle the task.

Several years ago I wrote a small poetry book entitled "A Heart Reflects." In it I wrote the following,

"Love bears its greatest fruit when the focus of its dedication is centered on forgiveness," and I dedicated it to everyone seeking to understand the way of peace. I concluded with this reminder, "Peace eludes those who leave forgiveness on the other side of the door of loving." Wasn't "forgiveness" one of the last sentiments held by Christ before he gave up his spirit? A glance around the world reveals a mightily shattered and splintered heart needing absolution. A question I often ask myself is, "Did I meet the full challenge of Jesus today, or did I only half love?"

Getting back to the Chapel of St. Mary Magdalene on the Via Doloroso, and after celebrating Mass that memorable morning, Father shared some of his personal feelings with our group. What he said in no way shocked me. "I must confess that during the Mass I just celebrated. I felt no sadness, only a peace and contentment I never thought I'd feel at the place where Jesus suffered so much." As I sat listening to him suddenly the words "Don't remember my pain, Linda, remember the gain" came to mind and from that moment I was resolute in looking beyond the cross and living faithfully the "resurrection" life. That was the task at hand — living a life that makes a difference for others.

There is one last and extremely important event that happened on the "Terra Santa" that had an intense effect on me and completely turned my head. Following a full day of lecturing and touring and after the evening meal, some members of the group would roam about the Old City savoring the sights until dusk. As for me, I would head over alone to the Church of the Holy Sepulcher and leisurely stroll about allowing my mind to wander and my eyes to absorb the visuals. I've discovered when visiting religious or historical sites it's best to have it talk to you rather that you to it. The Church of the Holy Sepulcher lends itself to reverence and silent attentiveness.

When you walk the Via Doloroso, the last five Stations of the Cross are in the Church of the Holy Sepulcher, built by Emperor Constantine at the request of his mother, Helena, in the fourth century. Tomes have been written about this unbelievable monument. My interest, however, was on the eleventh station — the site of the "Nailing of Jesus to the Cross." Upon entering the immense church and to the right of the Stone of Anointing — the place were Jesus' body was prepared for burial — are eighteen very steep steps leading up to the site of the Crucifixion. Literally, you are climbing up to the mound where Jesus was crucified. Reaching the top your eyes behold an array of visuals that is startling. First there is the Greek Orthodox Chapel with its icons, oil lamps and candles, where can be seen the Rock of Calvary. Directly to the right is the Roman Catholic Chapel of the Nailing to the Cross. The chapel's vaulted ceiling and magnificent large mosaic behind and above the

Medici altar hold the eye intently.

Within the large mosaic four figures are seen, as I can recall. In the forefront is Jesus, who having been impaled is lying upon the cross on the ground. His corpus is chalk white and wrapped only in a loin cloth. There's no evidence of blood oozing from any of the nail sites. His face appears impassive, and shows no emotion. One wonders if the artist's intent was to show that Jesus may have had the ability to place himself in a state of suspension, if only briefly, as he lay nailed to the cross. The faint shadow of the Roman soldier who impaled Jesus can be seen in the background clutching a hammer and spike.

The predominant figure in the scene is Mary, the Mother of Jesus. Wrapped in a dark cloak, standing at her son's left side, tall, solemn, serene and with hands clasped together, she appears to be gazing directly into another dimension as if absorbing the full reality of her Immaculate Conception that lies dying at her feet. Again, did the creator of the mosaic find it insufferable for Mary to watch as her son was ridiculed, taunted by the jeering crowd, stripped almost naked, and as a final blow witness his limbs run through with metal spikes? Did he in his compassion for the grief-stricken mother place her somewhere beyond the horrors of that human tragedy? Maybe, but who can know with certainty?

At the bottom of the cross crouched close to Jesus' body and painfully grieving is Mary Magdalene, who appears to be the only one grasping the grotesque brutality of the moment. Absolutely distraught over the horror of it all, the very human Magdalene lovingly rests her head next to the torso of the man who had set her free. One can imagine her crying out over and over, "Yeshua" "Yeshua! [Jesus], Why?" As is a woman's temperament to nurture, she grieves with an unexplained hope in her heart even as death encroaches. The woman from Magdala — the comforter, dedicated disciple, companion, and loving friend of the crucified — openly and unashamedly demonstrates her feelings for the man she obviously loved very much. Considering she was the only woman near the dying Jesus except for his mother, I wonder if the mosaic's designer sensed that the Magdalene's feelings were reciprocated by Jesus and that he wanted her close by to share the last moments of his life.

As I sat in that chapel on a hard wooden bench staring at that large piece of art, it became obvious to me that Mary Magdalene not only conveys by her comportment the tragedy of Calvary, but in her can be seen the embodiment of the true feminine. She is the personification of women everywhere who mourn the demise of what is good, tender-hearted, loving, and faithful. Her private and precious world had been extinguished by the aggressiveness of men choosing to expose the darker, more violent side of their nature as evidenced at Calvary. Trying to satisfy their need for dominance over the defenseless, such men have for eons plundered, raped, bludgeoned, coerced, and slaughtered the innocent. Possessing an insatiable appetite for manipulation, they seem incapable of tolerating a life spirited by love. Their solution? Expunge it! Kill it! And may truth be damned.

Bent over weeping, the Magdalene knew the condemned man was unlike others — not only because he was about to die for what he believed in, but for the "what-ness of his beliefs, beliefs that long after the cross would continue to set people free as she had been.

Over the three years that I brought people to the Holy Land, I sat in that chapel many, many times alone — absolutely alone. How that came about was unbelievable! One day I was introduced by our guide to a Greek Orthodox priest who tended the church. Being told I was a group leader, he recognized my need for private time and informed me that if I arrived a half-hour before the church was locked for the evening, he'd allow me to sit in the Chapel of the Nailing alone while he made his rounds checking that all pilgrims had left for the evening. Can you imagine climbing the steps leading to Calvary and spending more than thirty minutes alone at the spot where Jesus was crucified? Time after time I'd sit there feeling privileged to be in such *spirited* company. You really do get the sense the Heavenly Hosts are surrounding you.

Sitting alone in a dimmed room and not having

my thoughts interrupted by tourists scuffling about was formidable. Initially, I sat looking *at* the visual depictions in the mosaic but not *into* them. With eyes focused on it night after night, I began sensing that something was wrong. As beautiful as it was something was missing. It was the unidentifiable "something" that had me returning time and time again to sit there observing, reflecting, questioning, and denying. When I finally did discover the "something" I sat there grateful for another personal awakening.

Initially the Bible tells us little of the relationship between Mary Magdalene and Jesus. There is evidence in Gnostic texts, however, that he was seen by the other apostles as being outwardly affectionate towards her. Sitting all those hours in that Chapel contemplating her body language, I knew I had to personally come to some decision because it mattered to me what I believed. If in my mind I could see the possibility of such an occurrence, then what is the problem? Does such an assumption invalidate my allegiance to Christianity? I don't think so. Besides, since so little is known about the private years before his public ministry, wouldn't that make all or most of us "not in the know"? For me, it wasn't a time to cling to any prevailing belief or orthodoxy, nor was it a time for acceptance or denial; it was simply the awareness of a possibility I considered to be obvious. Such an insight makes Jesus' humanity appear to me more believable.

Walking out of the Church of the Holy Sepulcher for the last time, I glanced back at the mosaic and became absolutely convinced that more happened in the life of Jesus than was ever written. More was spoken than was ever recorded. Because of that I continue to listen intently to the sounds of my soul as it fills in between the lines.

Leaving Israel for the last time, I spent many hours reflecting on what I had learned and what I was made aware of. I believed from the bottom of my heart I had been sent there to absorb and understand more about a person I knew only through the Scriptures as Jesus. My insights into the personality of the man held great meaning for me. Whatever one holds Jesus to be — Son of God, Sage, Prophet, Healer, etc. —he was truly a remarkable human being who held steadfast to his intention to raise the consciousness of people. He fostered traits that made it possible for him to accomplish what he set out to do. Notably, he was an extraordinary decision maker, an attribute I consider paramount in a leader. His intention to serve was never compromised by any emotional inclination to do otherwise. He was firm and resolute in expressing his beliefs and making decisive decisions reflecting them. Like us, he too lived in a world that expressed itself through the duality of opposites. Yet being unwavering in his intention to lift the awareness of the people he met, he mindfully chose peace over aggression, love over hate, calm over anger, caring over indifference, pardon over blame, and acceptance over refusal. By the decisions he made, I can honestly say that Jesus gave his life for what he believed in long before he gave it up on the cross.

Jesus was acutely aware of the workings of the human psyche. With a few words of truth, he could move people to rethink their needs and replace old worn out thoughts with a newer vision of their desired wholeness. Remember what Jesus told the man after he healed him? "You are well now so stop sinning or something worse will happen to you." In other words Jesus was telling the man to hang up his old habits and replace them with actions that would affirm his new life, actions that wouldn't damage his body or diminish his spirit. I'm sure of one thing, Jesus wanted to change people's minds but to do that he had to reach their hearts. The best way to assure a change in heart is to lift a person's sagging and ailing spirit.

The one question I continued to ask myself was how could I be as effective as Jesus? Although there were differences, I knew there had to be sameness somewhere. One day it hit me. Jesus told his disciples they could do all he did and more. Initially, they certainly didn't seem to possess anything near what Jesus had. Yet look what they accomplished! What did he teach them? Was it classified information as part of a secret club we don't know about? I doubt that. I believe he taught them how to be spiritually attuned to the world and not just physically linked, and how to listen to the promptings of their inner spirit so they could accurately "read" the energy of others. Finally, they had to grasp the implication that if the Spirit of God created all things then in all things lay that same Spirit. Within the haughty and hurtful, the loving and the selfish, within all people and things, the Spirit of God is there. And they came to understand that God — the *Source of All That Is* — was not up there, over there or around there, but located at the very core of their being, within their soul where could be found the seat of their real power.

I often wonder how long it took the Apostles to trust in and utilize the creative energy of the Divine within them. One thing is for sure: by embracing the authentic truth of their nature and that of the Source within, they were able to continue the legacy of a man called Jesus.

13

In Search of a Place

The soul in its transition
seeks for the place
its deeds gain admission.

—Linda Luz Benvenue

New Visions made its last journey to the Holy Land in June, 1984. By then the situation in the Middle East was as critical as the one at the Blizzard household. What I'm going to relate is in consideration of all that had happened previously.

Wouldn't we all like to think we are infallible, incapable of making a mistake? Oh, if such were the reality of what is. Although you can hide the truth for years, eventually, it pushes to be recognized.

Throughout the early years when miracles abounded in our household, I was totally enveloped in being wife, mother, student, and teacher. Although my husband's indifference was problematic from the onset of our marriage, I kept its effects on me hidden for years. But as we got older, it became worse. After several years of family counseling it became apparent that the inevitable lay not too far ahead. I felt helpless at making things better. In August of 1983, I separated from John and with the children moved permanently to the Jersey Shore. After five years we were officially divorced, and John married again shortly thereafter. Unfortunately, he and his new bride had little time together. In December of 1991, he had a heart attack and died one week after undergoing heart by-pass surgery. Needless to say upon hearing of his death, we were all deeply saddened. He was a brilliant man who was still young —barely sixty-five, with a new wife, a new life, and little time left to dream. To this day I am grateful for the time we shared together.

Settling permanently in another state is always somewhat of a hassle. After I left John in 1983, I continued traveling to Pennsylvania twice weekly to teach at New Visions. However, after returning from Israel in 1984, my children were concerned about the dangers of me traveling back and forth to

Pennsylvania alone and asked if I would consider giving it up. It didn't take long to make my decision. Within one month News Visions came to an end.

Spending all my time with the children, who were in their mid-teens by then, was wonderful; however, I realized I would soon need something to do, but what? I considered volunteering at the local Catholic church and approached the pastor about beginning a scripture study program. He was delighted and suggested I write the Bishop of the Camden Diocese asking for permission and sending along my credentials. Approximately two weeks later I discovered that the pastor was being transferred to another parish so I decided to forego my endeavor for awhile — quite awhile.

As the days passed I became more listless and knew it was time to be productive. One night, before going to bed I said "Lord, that's it. Tomorrow morning I'm going to find a job in the newspaper. I don't care what it is. I need to do something." Not expecting a fanfare, I went to sleep with the words "I'm behind any door you choose" echoing in my brain. The next day I went down the list of available jobs. It didn't look good, but I was determined to find something. I was already down to the positions beginning with the letter "s" when I saw it. Sell furs! Mmm, I thought, I know nothing about furs, but I can learn. Yes, I can do that! I called the number listed and within two weeks found myself with a trunk load of furs, which I had paid several thousand dollars for.

This was going to be my first paying job since 1964 when I worked in Philly after divorcing John the first time.

The gentleman who owned the fur company told me, "The best way to make money is to sell them cheaper than anyone else. Instead of tripling or doubling the cost, why not charge one or two hundred dollars above the wholesale price? This way you're guaranteed to sell more." "Sounds good," I told him. "I'll give it a try." Not having a store, I held house parties at different homes schlepping the furs in the trunk of my car. Luckily I did pretty well and within a year had a small room in a realty company from which to sell my goods. I was meeting people and having fun.

Eventually, I was bitten by the retail bug and took a gamble at opening a small boutique in Brigantine, New Jersey selling women's clothing, jewelry, and accessories. I called the store Maggie Jones Boutique.

Selling furs was one thing but selling an array of merchandise was challenging. To begin with, I had absolutely no idea how to go about finding the goods to sell. Luckily, a friend who had a business in town told me about a buying show held in New York at the Coliseum. Together we traipsed up to the Big City amazed at what we saw. My problem was I had a limited budget and no idea what my future clientele would like. Plus, even if I wanted to order something, I had no idea how to fill out the purchasing order.

Feeling stupid but trying to look like I was "in the know" I walked around observing how other buyers placed their orders, but it still wasn't sinking in. Finally, I sat down in a booth and being totally frustrated asked a salesman if he would show me how to fill out an order form and explain some of the garment jargon. After a fifteen-minute lesson, I was on my own. It was all so exciting; I really enjoyed it! Even in this venture God was always close by. Before each buying trip I'd pray, "Lord, please help me to choose what is best for my ladies." He always did and everybody loved their purchases. My daughter Linda came on board and we worked side by side for years.

I have to say, Maggie Jones Boutique was not that different than New Visions. Instead of selling the "Good News" to cover their souls, I simply switched to selling clothes to cover their bodies. It's amazing how special and unique each one of my customers was. With their own story to tell, I'd listened as they'd speak about their recent cancer or their husband's. We'd cry together when they talked about their parents' Alzheimer's or the sudden death of a child. Feeling helpless, it wasn't long before I started handing out inspirational cards to those who needed a little hope and support along the way. The sentiments on the card were a simple reminder of the truth. "Lord, help me to remember that nothing is going to happen to me today that you and I together cannot handle." Over the years I would say that my employees and I handed out hundreds to women needing a hug and a spiritual hand.

As I review the nineties, I have to say they were productive but very challenging years. A gamut of emotions flooded those years, ranging from great elation to unbelievable sadness. First I was honored to be asked to be on the school board of our local public school, a position I held until 1998. Then in 1993 it was time for a big wedding. My daughter Linda and her fiancé Paul were to be married in October. However, in August several months prior to the wedding my mom passed away. At the exact moment of her death I had a major heart attack at her bedside in the hospital. Seeing her take her last breath I let out a gasp and instantly felt the most god-awful pain in my chest. Thankfully, my brother Manny and my sister-in-law Pat were there.

Initially I said nothing to either of them about the discomfort. It wasn't until I became nauseous that I mentioned how I was feeling. Manny offered to take me down to the Emergency Room to be checked out, but I wasn't about to consider the possibility of becoming a patient in the very hospital where my mom's body was lying in the morgue. We all agreed that watching her pass away probably caused the acid in my stomach to churn, accounting for the pain. After ten minutes we left the hospital and returned to Brigantine to tell my dad the sad news. Gratefully, by then my entire family had moved to the shore from Pennsylvania, including my parents and brother. When we reached my dad's home the pain was getting worse. I can remember pushing my fist into the middle of my chest trying to hold in the pain as my dad and I cried in each other's arms.

That night I went to bed with my daughter rubbing my arm for hours until I finally feel asleep. When I awoke the next morning I felt as if someone had tied a block of concrete to both legs. That's when I thought that maybe it was more than my stomach. I asked my son Jeffrey to take me to see a friend of mine who was a physician in Ventnor. After taking an EKG, he told me, "Linda, you are in the middle of a heart attack; you must go immediately to the emergency room at Atlantic City Hospital." "Doctor Ron, I can't go to the hospital, I'm sorry; I have to bury my mom." In a flash he called my son into his office and said, "If you don't take your mom right now to the hospital, Jeffrey, you are going to bury two members of your family, not one." Within a half an hour I was admitted to the coronary intensive care unit of Atlantic City Hospital, where I was diagnosed as having suffered a myocardial infarction that had damaged my heart muscle.

Lying in the hospital trying to believe I had a heart attack at the moment of my mom's death was incomprehensible. In fact, every time I gave it more than a moment's thought the pain would return. My mom, who had died on a Thursday, was to be buried in Pennsylvania on Monday. When I asked the doctors for permission to go, they informed me that on Monday I would be going by ambulance to Graduate Hospital in Philadelphia for testing — which is exactly what happened. It was there they discovered that my heart attack was not the result of clogged arteries but due to observing the process of death. My heart muscle literally contracted as my mom took her final breath. Sadly, I never did get to bury my mom.

14

Moving Ahead

Away death!
Let me flee!
Someone has opened
a new door for me.

—Linda Luz Benvenue

After a six-month recuperative period, my life took on a new direction. I have always believed that if there is a special task the Lord wants you to do, you can be sure he'll bring it to you via other people. When that happens there's no doubt it's yours to do; it has your name written all over it. In the spring of 1994, I was visited in my place of business by the pastor from our church asking if I would consider heading a program for the parish. Of course, I was delighted but wondered— since he didn't really know me—how he was sure I had the credentials to do the job. Well, as it turned out his wonderful secretary, Rosemary Petti, remembered me calling the parish several years prior when I was considering volunteering. She mentioned my name to him and the rest fell into place. For the next ten years, I dedicated myself to the island church of Saint Thomas the Apostle knowing full well the Lord had directed me there through my dear friend, Rosemary, and I was under his employ.

Fortunately during those years my daughter, who was married by this time, and another employee, Mary Chisholm, had things pretty much under control at Maggie Jones Boutique, which left me free to devote most of my time helping to establish Diocesan programs at the parish and to facilitate the development of parish ministries. How fortunate I was to have worked with three different pastors who trusted in my ability to help them move the parish forward. Thankfully, that allowed me to fulfill the work God had placed me there to do.

St. Thomas the Apostle Church is set just a few hundred yards off the beach. Its Spanish architecture gives it an Old World charm that I loved and still do. One my greatest privileges was meeting and working with so many wonderful people who eagerly embraced all visitors to the island church. The other was having dubbed the church "the beacon on the beach," which it truly is. Its visibility near the water continues to light the way for those wandering the beach looking for the "Son." The members of that small parish community should be very proud as they continue to remain committed to the Gospel message. I am not being corny here, believe me. The parish, as with any parish, had a conglomeration of personalities, including those of the priests, that at times made it difficult to move forward. But when the awareness of why we had gathered resurfaced, we'd all inch ahead making progress once again. Whenever projected goals became a reality, I'd often sit in the back of the church thinking "how'd we do that?" knowing all along that a spirit of discipleship was alive and doing well at the little beacon church.

Volunteering and giving retreats at St. Thomas was definitely a full-time job. By the mid-nineties all the kids were either married or living on their own and I was OK with living alone. Then one day out of the blue I happened to mention to my daughter's mother-in-law, Pat, that I'd like to find a really good man at some point. Well, one very cold, snowy night in February, she suggested that after our workout at the gym we all go to the Rod 'n' Reel for dinner. This included my daughter and her husband and his parents. The "Rod" is a local tavern specializing in billiards, beer, and some food on the side. My initial reaction was "I'm not going there!" Her husband, Don, dittoed my response. "Oh yes you are, follow me," she said. So off we traipsed to the "Rod."

What was unknown to me was that Pat had a man in mind she wanted me to meet and arranged a blind encounter that night with him and another couple he often dined with. When the five of us arrived we sat down and ordered our dinners. About a half-hour later in walks the mystery man and his friends. After we were introduced they sat at another table for dinner. I thought nothing of it until the wife of the couple invited us to come and join them. That's when I had my first clue that something just might be brewing. Walking over to the table I happened to sit next to the couple's friend, Andy.

Talk about feeling awkward! There I was sitting next to this tall, lean, handsome stranger wearing a bright yellow jacket and brown corduroy pants. Not knowing what to say, I spoke to everyone else at the table but him. Then he looked at me and asked what I did. Well, if I tell you we talked for about an hour straight, I wouldn't be exaggerating. He was a widower and though I was divorced, I basically felt the same since John had passed away. When it was time to leave we walked towards the door and together paused in the doorway briefly sensing the closeness of the other's presence. It was magical! Anyway, we said good-bye and walked into the snowy night to our cars never knowing if we'd see each other again. "Well, how about that!" I thought to myself, he didn't even ask for my phone number."

About three o'clock the following afternoon, which was a Saturday, the doorbell rang and there standing at my front door holding the biggest bouquet of flowers I ever saw was our local florist with a hugh grin on his face. Handing me the flowers I had no idea who they might be from. As I opened them a card dropped out and I read the following, "It was a pleasure meeting you last night. I only hope my life turns out as great as yours." It was simply signed "Andy." Still there was no "I'll call you" or "see you soon," nothing! I was confused. Should I call and thank him for the flowers or just send a brief note inviting him over to see the them in full bloom? I chose the former. Unfortunately, I was really disappointed. He never said one word or hinted at wanting to see me again. Oh well, that's the way it goes sometimes. But I did love the flowers and really did want to see him again.

On Wednesday of the following week about seven in the evening the phone rang. It was Andy asking me for a date. I think the conversation lasted all of three minutes. I said "yes" and on Friday of that week we had a great time dining at a wonderful restaurant. We talked so much we literally closed the place that night. The date was February 9, 1996. From that night on we saw each other every day and in less than a week on Valentine's Day he asked, "Would you ever consider marrying again?" I nodded, and he asked "Well, would you ever consider marrying me?" I nodded again and that was that. I knew it was as right as the hand on my arm. The good man I was looking for had arrived.

Needless to say everyone was shocked we had made such a quick decision. But Andy was sixty and I wasn't far behind. We knew what we wanted and saw no reason to wait. We were married in Bermuda on September 13 of that year. We will be married eleven years this coming September. Every February third, my wonderful husband sends me a beautiful bouquet of flowers — never missing once. Three days ago, which was the third, a card came tucked inside the bouquet that said, "With you my years have all turned out great." He had remembered again.

When I first met Andy, my dad wasn't faring very well. His health was and had been in jeopardy for years. Being a considerate person Andy suggested he live with us after we were married. How wonderful that would be. I was delighted. Regretfully, my dad passed away in June just months before we were to wed in September. Of this I can say with certainty: My dad wasn't about to leave this earth until I had met the right man. Knowing Andy for only several months he knew he had met the man he could entrust his daughter with. In fact, on the day he died a nurse in the hospital jokingly asked him what such a handsome young man was doing in the hospital. To that my dad replied, "My daughter's getting married and I have places to go now." Little did I know that four hours after hearing him say those words, he'd be gone. Yes, I believe my dad held off going to that "other place" until he was sure I'd be happy and no longer alone. What a great dad he was. I still miss him a lot.

After Andy and I were married, I continued volunteering at the church and working at my business. It's ironic how the same feeling that draws you to something also draws you away when it's time to move on. We had talked about the possibility of moving out of Brigantine at some point and buying a home with some land. It was around that time I sensed that the job I was sent to do at the church was finished. With no obstacles except for Maggie Jones, it would be a good time to sell our island home in Brigantine, New Jersey. In November of 2003, that's exactly what we did. We moved to the mainland where we found a wonderful place on seven acres of land. After all these years I found myself roaming the woods once again.

Life was perfect for us. Although I still had to travel almost daily to Maggie Jones, which was fifteen miles away, it was a joy coming home to my husband, and the deer and turkeys we shared the property with. Outside of working at my store, I spent a lot of time contemplating what I would do next. After all the years as a retailer, I wanted more than anything to be free of that burden and return to giving motivational talks and "reality" retreats. Also in the back of my mind was the idea of writing a book about my spiritual experiences, which I felt God was prompting me to do. When my daughter informed me she was pregnant and wouldn't be able to work any longer, I knew the time for Maggie Jones was dwindling. It wasn't long before I learned the consequences of pushing my endurance beyond its limit.

From April until August of 2005 with only myself and Mary, and my cousin Eileen, who filled in when she could, I was stressed, tired, aggravated, and feeling depression at my heels. Eileen had mentioned several times that I didn't look quite good but as usual I paid little attention to her insight. On August nineteenth I awoke with such severe pains in my chest I immediately thought I was having another heart attack. However, this time a virus had planted itself on the lining of my heart causing it to swell and my lungs to fill with fluid. Besides developing all kinds of peripheral problems, I had great difficulty breathing without pain. This went on for months, during which time I was hospitalized twice and diagnosed as having pericarditis with bilateral pleural effusions. I knew I was extremely ill.

Several days after my final release from the hospital, I was home walking down our hall corridor, still in pain, when I suddenly had the feeling that my next breath would find me on the next level of my journey. Needless to say I am not a ghost writer; nothing happened. But for the first time, I felt no terror or fear of death, just the awareness that it was about to happen and I had to allow it. It was as if I had to give death permission to intrude. Actually, there wasn't any time left for many other thoughts.

That afternoon I told my husband that if anything happened to me I wanted an autopsy performed. You have to understand I never, ever, would have said anything like that before. I was caught up in life with too much to do to let death interfere. After all, I had already had a heart attack at fifty-five and survived. But this time doubt crept into my thoughts and I had no choice but to recognize the moment for what is was — total surrender.

About one week after the above experience, I was feeling somewhat better and at breakfast told Andy of the incident and that I was certain someone's hand had held me back from moving beyond the present into the next plane of perceptions. At that exact moment, the kitchen lights began to flicker off and on for no apparent reason. We checked the clocks, the lights, and other appliances to make sure they hadn't stopped. All were functioning fine. Nothing was askew. The morning was beautiful with not a cloud in the sky. Andy and I looked at each other knowing that in that instant someone — some higher consciousness — was letting me know my suspicions were correct. As I see it now, my body was headed for the exit door, but my spirit wasn't ready to comply. Doesn't it say in scripture that it's when Jesus gave up his spirit that he died? After a year and a half my spirit and my body are now fully recovered and in sync. In March of 2006, I finally sold Maggie Jones Boutique.

15

Then Came The Dawn

It's not our intentions that fail us,
but our inclinations that nail us.

—Linda Luz Benvenue

After my encounter with pericarditis in 2005, I knew it was time to give a little more thought to the rest of my earthly sojourn. There's no doubt that for me life is a ten-minute journey. Such awareness tends to keep me spiritually focused. As I see it, if each moment is equivalent to about nine years, I may have about two and a half minutes left on my corporal clock, give or take a few seconds. The experiences I wrote about in this memoir took up almost eight of those minutes. It doesn't take much thought to wonder what I'd like to do with my remaining moments — lots and lots, and I'm hoping the Lord has them all booked.

To begin with I see myself now as a "spirit in waiting." Waiting to sing the song of my spirit that is alive and well in me. There is an exuberance being spiritually uninhibited knowing that I'm loved unreservedly and totally as Jesus was and nothing can change that. God went to great lengths to make sure I was certain of that. No longer do I need to feel disloyal if I question the validity of things considered off limits. If I choose to deny what some hold as absolute truth, it's OK and not punishable by death as was the case with my Jewish Jesus. If I discern through prayer or simply by talking with God that a decision I make is right for me but contrary to the religious norm, it's OK. After all, I have consulted in truth and honesty with a higher authority. If I become aware of any bigotry I might hold then I best beware! If I believe my way to be the only way, then maybe I've gotten in God's way. If I can express my pain and disappointments honestly to the Source of All within me, no matter how absurd they may seem, then I'm allowing myself to be bathed in the restorative powers of the Divine. Again, how great is that!

Over the years there were two remaining issues that gripped my soul, leading to distraction that needed resolution. First, several years ago I heard a priest say during his homily that if Jesus didn't resurrect from the dead there would be no need to believe in Him and that such a nonoccurrence would make Christianity null and void. What a shocker that was! I want to say I totally, passionately, and wholeheartedly disagree with that man. I respect his opinion and those of others believing the same. I have a "holy" other view of the man who loved and embraced mankind and tried to teach it how to love soulfully.

Personally, I observed from Jesus' encounters with people that forgiveness isn't just a vocabulary word but a genuine act of healing, a true act of kindness. Through his teachings, I learned how to spark my sagging spirit allowing it to flourish once again. By his guidance I was shown how to look at the simple and behold the Divine. He showed me the joy in sharing the truth of me with family and friends. It was from a not so simple "preacher man" who lived over two millennia ago that I discovered how to delight in the beauty of all creation and its creatures — those that fly and those that crawl. By example, I continue to allow myself quiet moments each day to reflect on God's way for me. It's the *living of his life* that inspires me and not the way he met his death as terrible and tragic as it was. As far as rising from the dead? He taught me how to rise above those things that can easily hold me to the cross, like self-absorption, pride, deviousness, malice, and an unforgiving heart, to name but a few. Jesus, my spiritual partner with whom I am conjoined, reminds me that with him I can always go on for one minute more. If I have any doubt of that, I simply cock my head and hear him say, "Psst, Linda, over here, follow me."

The other issue I finally resolved happened when I walked into my little church by the ocean, knelt down in a pew and with my head lowered, said, "Jesus, I want you to know I love you from the bottom of my heart. It is this love that brings me here today to admit what is deeply troubling me. There is uncertainty in my heart as to some of the things they have written about you. I want you to know my love doesn't depend on whether you rose from the dead or not, as many contend it should. I love you for leaving me a trove of sacred treasures to live by. I love you for being there each and every day listening to my woes, as well as my dreams and desires. But, most importantly, you have impressed upon this soul the certainty that all things created by the Source of All will continue to expand into realms that lay beyond this earth, and life will continue to flourish both in and beyond the now moment in ways I cannot ever imagine or presume. And, I will be part of it all. For that I gratefully and joyously thank you.

I knelt there quietly for awhile before I raised my head, looked directly at the cross above the altar, and whispered, "And now, my dear Jesus, teacher, and friend, I have come to take you down from the cross." Kneeling there with tears running down my face and onto my chest, I placed my hands out in front of me and allowed the image of his weakened body — now resting in my arms — to seep into every cell of my body. As I did, I knew immediately that his love had set me free to live the rest of my life without guilt or feelings of complicity. Slowly, I got up from the pew and said, "OK, my friend, it's time to leave now. It's a beautiful day and I think a walk on the beach is in order for both of us."

Walking slowly out of the church I savored each moment as I sauntered down the aisle with a feeling of liberation that brought a smile to my face and a tug at my heart. My small frame seemed to grow in leaps and bounds as I raised my head feeling ten feet tall. As I got closer to the door, I had the feeling that someone's arm was wrapped tightly around mine. Approaching the exit I took a deep breath and said, "After you, my Lord, after you." Walking out into the sunlight and onto the sandy beach, which was steps away, I had the feeling I was back in Galilee walking near its shores listening to Jesus tell me how precious I am to him. Likewise, Lord, likewise.

With those issues personally resolved, I can say without hesitation that each event that happened in my life has been a dawning — the emergence of a new light penetrating my spirit, giving me courage to face the unknown of each day. Its voice is distinguishable, its sound detectable within the crevices of my being. I listen, I hear, I acknowledge Presence. Once again there is union at its most profound level as the words "Come and see" draw me ever closer. As usual, the Lord makes us an offer we can't refuse. Listen for it!

I would like to share with you a prayer I was inspired to write as I completed this spiritual memoir. I say it daily. It's the three "R's" of spiritual awakening — rethink, refocus, replace.

> The Dawning
>
> Today, I choose to pursue my goodness and empty my heart of things that do not reflect the magnitude of my creation.
>
> Light of Truth, illuminate the Divine mystery that I am. Take me to where you speak to my soul so I can uncover the boldness I need to **rethink** old habits that stifle my goodness; to **refocus** on the delights of life and not the distractions; and to **replace** thoughts that hinder with those that help.
>
> I know Divine Truth embraces me always with with infinite compassion. I am grateful to be so richly blessed.

May the Source of ALL THAT IS bless you and may its light shine through you revealing your own godlike divinity.

16

Afterword
A Personal Reflection

Believe strongly in your imaginings;
your tomorrows depend on it.
—Linda Luz Benvenue

Throughout my life religion has been important to me. Through it I discovered a plethora of names for God and "other worldly" deities and how to pray to them. I learned about the Ten Commandments and the Beatitudes, as well as the different parts of the Mass and how to pray the rosary, etc. In my capacity as a human I knew enough religious practices to keep me busy for the rest of my life. But was "busy" what

I really wanted? No! And how many prayers did I have to say before I felt a bit closer to God, maybe ten, maybe twenty? I was never sure. It was that uncertainty that made me vulnerable to continue searching for that "it" that appeared to be missing.

Having focused on my physical nature for years, I knew its limitations. When I had my hysterectomy and still wanted to feel "what it was like" to bear a child, you can be sure I was definitely going way beyond my limitation — I was asking for the impossible! Yet it happened — minus one small detail. My daughter was born from my heart and not from my belly even though the entire setting was that of a delivery experience as you read. She was born out of a desire that went way beyond the physical. When I heard the words that night in the hospital "You wanted to know what it was like" I knew I had discovered something within myself capable of doing the impossible. Someone or something was letting me know *it* had heard my request and went to great lengths to comply.

Likewise at Fatima, my spirit was as down as it could be and then the words came "I know you are here." Who or what was mimicking what I had said hours before? All I knew was my disappointment was being acknowledged. Over and over it seemed that I was being validated by a something that was continually moving within me waiting to respond to the needs of my spirit.

Reflecting on the events of my life I knew it was time for me to come up with a clearer definition of God, as I know him to be in my life. Early on it was obvious that he had found me because I was there to be found. Anyway, I started out very simply by remembering what I had been taught when I was a child, that God who created everything was located in heaven. In the early days of my religious formation, that was all I was capable of absorbing. Thinking beyond the obvious wasn't expected of me at that time, so I relied on what I was told was truth. Likewise, I couldn't grasp the nature of my inner spirit so I simply focused on physical survival. OK, if God is in heaven then he is beyond the limitations of earth, meaning I am dealing with less specificity so the personification of God has to give way to "something else." It was that "something else" that seemed so distant and unclear.

Eventually I came to the conclusion that no where in the universe — not on this planet, or in any church or philosophical institution — can God be defined. He is indefinable, yet at the same time more knowable than we can imagine. In praying I feel the forces of love penetrate me; in injury I sense the force of compassion healing me. There is a force within me making me aware of myself. Is that force God? Is it a "he," "she," or "it" force? Is this the source from which all forces have their origin such as the force of good and that of love? Because we are more spiritually evolved today than the people of Jesus' time, are we better able to respond to and grasp a newer vision of "who God is" or should the interrogative be "what"? To say that the Force of all forces, the Fundamental Force within the "all that is," is God is certainly a bit more complex than saying God is a Divine being residing in a place called heaven. However, maybe the former is easier to understand than the latter since science has already demonstrated that all matter is made up of energy.

Whatever the answer I think God may want to be known and understood in ways that are more universal and more out-reaching for today's space traveler. If God is the Ultimate, the Primary, the Fundamental Creative force behind, through and in everything, then am I not a tangible form of that reality just as Jesus was? Are we not all visible forms of a God Force? Another way of saying that is the Force that created the universe, of which I am a part, is one with me and vice versa. Its energy runs through every cell of my being. It's the energy connecting my spirit to the All That Is.

At first I thought it rather cold and impersonal talking about God as a force instead of a Divine entity, mainly because the former brings to mind an impersonal energy while the latter connotes a caring being. I was happy knowing God was a Divine being in heaven looking down on me. I liked the personal aspect of having Jesus as my brother. But if God is up there and I'm down here then that implies separation. That cannot be. I remember wishing at times I could pick up the phone and dial up God. It would make things so much easier. However, I think my problem would lie in the connection, and I'd keep repeating the words spoken on that grinding TV commercial, "Can you hear me now?"

Several months ago while revisiting the words spoken by Jesus, I suddenly became aware of the dynamics contained within one verse found in the Gospels of Luke and Mark. "When you pray and ask for something, believe that you have received it, and you will be given whatever you ask for." (Luke 11:14) Bingo! With those words no wonder the apostles could replicate what Jesus did. He taught them how to use the God energy within themselves to heal others. He showed them how to envision wholeness and not fragmentation. And no wonder Jesus could say "the Father and I are one." He recognized his connectedness to Universal Force (God). In other words there was no fragmentation of the fundamental energy within Jesus.

When I peruse scripture now I'm amazed at the many ways he taught us to keep the pure energy of the Divine Source positively flowing in us so we could maintain a good connection with it. Basically, he taught us how to go with the rhythm of the Force. When I read the New Testament now, in light of the above, my mind is blown away by the manner in which Jesus tried to teach the people about a reality they couldn't possibly have grasped at that time. In a roundabout way wasn't he telling them the truth? For example, instead of using the word "Force" or "Energy," he used the word "Father." And when he spoke about the dangers of sinning could it be he was simply pointing out the consequences of diluting our energy by holding onto attitudes associated with the material world like greed, jealousy, envy, pride, etc.? Living with a watered down rendition of the Source energy makes us susceptible to walking a crooked road and experiencing a myriad of other unpleasant conditions that could affect our mind, our body, and our spirit.

Do our selfish motives bring about the evils that beset the world? As far as I see it, yes. To me the fundamental creative energy is pure consciousness, pure light composed of all that is good, kind, loving, and selfless. Nothing within "it" is evil. We as humans, I suspect because of our egos, manipulate the forces and bring that about ourselves. However, there is one action Jesus talks about that may help reestablish our connectedness to the All That Is and that is to "forgive anything you may have done against anyone." Does an unforgiving heart walk in darkness because it chooses not to restore its connection to the Forces of Light and truth? Does fragmentation become the shoe that fits? Figuratively speaking, Jesus moved us from the Dark Ages into the Age of Light.

Finally, how far do the words "ask and believe you have received it," go? If we absolutely trust with a *knowing* trust that through our connectedness to the "Source of All" we will receive exactly what we request, is it not possible to ask to die a peaceful death — and believe it will happen? Can I project now what I want to happen to my spirit when it leaves this plane of awareness? So many questions for certain, but I'm sure they'll all be answered at some point in universal time.

In the meantime, being as human as ever and a creature of habit, when I pray and talk with the Divine Force I still say "Our Father who art in Heaven. . . ." Nothing has changed except I now see myself as a vessel containing the primal forces of the universe, allowing me to use its power for good and to teach others to do likewise. It was a long search but well worth it, especially since I found "It" to be not only powerful but also very personal to me.

There is a mantra I wrote and say daily to remind me of my inherited power. It's very empowering! By taking the first letter from each word in "All That Is, Lives In Me," the acronym formed is "ATILIM" (pronounced Ah-Tee-Leem with the accent on "leem"). When I say "leem," allowing the humming sound of the "m" to resonate and linger for a few seconds, I begin to feel empowered by the reality of its truth. The awareness that I am one with the All That Is, is incredible! The perception that I am conjoined with the Divine and capable of giving it creative expression is both humbling and numbing. Whenever I reflect on the meaning of this mantra, I'm reminded of the awesome responsibility I have to embrace all that lies under the umbrella of Divine creation. The only way I know how to do that is to make gratitude the sentiment of my heart and compassion the sword of my soul.

I would like to end this spiritual memoir by quoting once again Maya Angelou's beautiful insight into why a bird sings: "A bird does not sing because it has an answer, it sings because it has a song." Like the cooing dove, you and I carry within us a distinguishable sound that makes us identifiable from others. However, with the awareness that the "all that is" lives in me, in you, and in all things, we can now join our feathered friends in singing boldly the Ballad of Oneness.... "There is no here, no there, no then or now. There is no time, no space. There is a me in Thee and that is WHO AM."

A Personal Note from the Author

If you have had a "dawning" experience of your own, I invite you to consider sharing that with me. The impact of your experience could help others. For privacy purposes it can be written anonymously, or if you choose to have your testimony considered for inclusion in the next "Dawning" book or placed on my website, be sure to add the following statement to your disclosure: I (your name), give Linda Luz Benvenue permission to use my testimony for the purpose of enlightening others. Please send your testimony to: info@thedawningexperience.com

For information regarding availability for speaking engagements and the latest updates to the "dawning" please visit my website at: www.thedawningexperience.com

About the Author

As a motivational speaker, Linda Luz Benvenue, has for the past twenty-six years given lectures and "reality" retreats to help people understand the synergy and collaboration that exists between divine/spirit awareness and human/ego consciousness. With clarity and compassion, she teaches and offers ways individuals can move from being credible to incredible, ordinary to extraordinary, knowing they possess the inherent power to make it happen. In understanding the differences that exists in living a life directed by the intentions of the spirit, or one lived solely to satisfy the inclinations of the ego, a person can stand either atop the mount of freedom creating a life that matters, or be always at the bottom looking up, wishing. She believes that many of life's hesitations often arise out of the tension that exists between the two.

www.ingramcontent.com/pod-product-compliance
Ingram Content Group UK Ltd.
Pitfield, Milton Keynes, MK11 3LW, UK
UKHW041847190726
13854UKWH00002B/760

9 781425 128548